A YOUNG PERSON'S GUIDE to PHILOSOPHY

"I THINK, THEREFORE I AM"

philosophy *meaning love of wisdom*
from the Greek philos *(loving or dear)* and sophia *(wisdom or knowledge)*

CONSULTANT EDITOR: JEREMY WEATE
ILLUSTRATED BY PETER LAWMAN

DK PUBLISHING, INC.
www.dk.com

A DK PUBLISHING BOOK

Editor Linda Esposito
Art Editor Diane Thistlethwaite
Editorial Assistance Jennifer Siklós
US Editor Constance Robinson

Production Josie Alabaster
Picture Researchers
James Clarke and Martin Redfern
Jacket Design
Sophia Tampakopoulos

Commissioned illustrations
conceived and designed by
Diane Thistlethwaite and Linda Esposito

Philosophy Consultant
Dr. Sharon Ney

Specialist Advice
Dr. Lilian Alweiss, Dr. Mike Beany,
Dr. R. Blaug, Dr. P. J. FitzPatrick,
Prof. Steve Jackson, Dr. Matthew Kieran,
Dr. John Schwarzmantel

First American Edition, 1998
2 4 6 8 10 9 7 5 3

Published in the United States by
DK Publishing, Inc.
95 Madison Avenue, New York, NY 10016

Visit us on the World Wide Web at http://www.dk.com

Copyright © 1998
Dorling Kindersley Limited, London

Published in Great Britain by
Dorling Kindersley Limited.

Library of Congress Cataloging-in-Publication Data
Weate, Jeremy
    A young person's guide to philosophy: "I think, therefore I
am" / Jeremy Weate -- 1st American ed.
    p.   cm.
    Summary: Introduces over twenty-five of the world's greatest
philosophers and presents a simple version of the tenets of
philosophy.
    ISBN 0-7894-3074-6
    1. Philosophy--Juvenile literature. 2. Philosophers--Juvenile
literature. [1. Philosophy. 2. Philosophers.] I. Title. II. Title:
Guide to philosophy.
BD31.W43 1998
100--DC21
                                            97-33454
                                                 CIP
                                                  AC

Color reproduction by GRB Editrice S.r.l., Verona, Italy
Printed and bound in Italy by LEGO

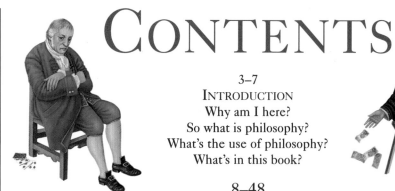

CONTENTS

WHY AM I HERE?
AM I DREAMING?
WHAT IS GOOD AND BAD?
HOW DID THE WORLD BEGIN?
IS THERE A GOD?

IF YOU HAVE EVER ASKED YOURSELF ANY OF THESE QUESTIONS, THEN YOU ARE on your way to becoming a philosopher. A philosopher is somebody who is puzzled by the world, and then asks questions about it. Although we all wonder about the unknown, some people have explored it more single-mindedly than others. Those people who are called great philosophers actually challenge and alter the way we think. Because of this, we remember them.

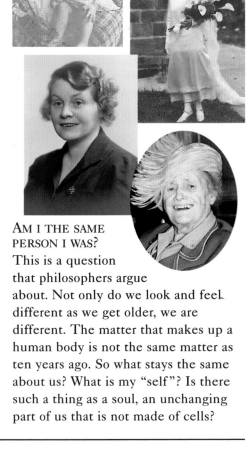

AM I THE SAME PERSON I WAS? This is a question that philosophers argue about. Not only do we look and feel different as we get older, we are different. The matter that makes up a human body is not the same matter as ten years ago. So what stays the same about us? What is my "self"? Is there such a thing as a soul, an unchanging part of us that is not made of cells?

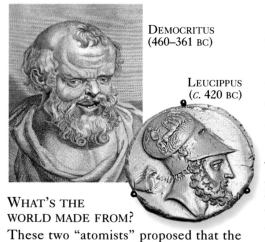

DEMOCRITUS
(460–361 BC)

LEUCIPPUS
(c. 420 BC)

WHAT'S THE WORLD MADE FROM?
These two "atomists" proposed that the world was made up of tiny particles. The atom was not discovered until 1803.

EARLY VEGETARIAN
Philosophy can change the way people lead their lives. Pythagoras (see p. 10) believed that all animals had souls. He and his followers refused to eat meat.

SO WHAT IS PHILOSOPHY?

PHILOSOPHERS RARELY AGREE ABOUT THIS. HOWEVER IT IS POSSIBLE TO GIVE GENERAL GUIDELINES. Philosophy begins with a sense of wonder at the world – when we no longer take things for granted. We question how things are. Philosophy explores what we don't know. When answers are found, philosophy becomes science. Science is about what we know, and how we know it. The difference between science and philosophy is that philosophy suggests ideas about what is not known. As times change there are always new questions.

WHEN DID IT ALL START?

It would be fair to say that people have always asked themselves questions about the world they live in. There probably have been great philosophers that we know nothing about, because their ideas were never recorded. Every society has had its own philosophers, whose ideas reflect their individual cultures. Their teachings have led to different traditions of philosophy, such as "Eastern," "Western," or "African."

This book explores the history of Western philosophy, which grew up in Europe over 2,500 years ago. The first great Western philosophers lived in what is today Greece, Italy, and Turkey (see pages 8–11). At that time there was a lot of sea trade between countries around the Mediterranean coast, which led to an exchange of ideas. These early thinkers were influenced by Egyptian and Babylonian ideas, so the roots of Western philosophy can be found in Africa.

WOLE SOYINKA (BORN 1934)
This Nigerian philosopher and dramatist won the Nobel Prize for Literature in 1984. His ideas often got him into trouble, and he has been exiled and imprisoned.

CONFUCIUS (551–479 BC)
This great Eastern philospher taught that the order of society is a natural order. People should accept their role in life, be it ruler or slave. His main teaching was "Do as you would be done by." He is known for his sayings, such as "A good man is never alone."

NICOLAS COPERNICUS (1473–1543)
A few early Greek philosophers had proposed that the Earth orbited the Sun. Copernicus's book *De Revolutionibus Orbium Celestrium* also stated this. The Church strongly opposed this idea.

DEATH OF SAVONAROLA, FLORENCE
In the past it was dangerous to question God's existence. The 15th-century Italian philosopher Savonarola was burned at the stake for his unconventional views.

WHAT'S THE USE OF PHILOSOPHY?

PHYSICS, CHEMISTRY, BIOLOGY, AND EVEN MATHEMATICS ALL USED TO BE PART OF PHILOSOPHY. BUT as technology advanced, philosophy and science separated. So what is the use of philosophy today? In fact, philosophers are much sought after, since they are trained to think clearly about problems. Newspapers and other media often ask their opinions about current topics. Even governments, hospitals, museums, and architects seek their advice.

Many philosophers work in universities, teaching young people how to think and argue clearly by studying other philosophers. The following questions are examples of those that philosophers ask today.

IS A COMPUTER VIRUS ALIVE?

Many philosophers use issues like computer viruses to question what life really is. There are many similarities between a computer virus and a human virus. A computer virus can spread from computer to computer, just as the flu, for instance, can spread from person to person. A computer virus can lie in a computer without being active, just as a person can have a virus and not be aware of it. A human virus is a string of coded information surrounded by proteins. A computer virus is also coded information, stored by electricity. The difference becomes even smaller when we consider that proteins are made up of atoms, which are electrically charged.

Philosophers argue that life can be defined as information passing itself on. A computer virus is information that reproduces itself. Humans reproduce themselves via information stored in their genes.

SCREEN SHOWING VIRUS DAMAGE

COMPUTER VIRUS
A computer virus is a program that destroys stored information. It can enter a computer's memory and copy itself until the memory is used up.

HUMAN VIRUS
As a separate unit, a virus shows no sign of life. But when a virus invades a living cell it can copy itself by hijacking the cell's chemical machinery.

VIRUS ATTACKING A CELL, VIEWED THROUGH AN ELECTRON MICROSCOPE

AM I AN ANDROID?

Is this really such a silly question? Androids were once the stuff of science fiction. Now technology is catching up. One day it may well be possible to create a machine that looks and thinks like a human. It could even be programmed to "feel" emotion. And what if that android didn't know it was a machine…? Philosophers are interested in artificial intelligence because some think it is only a matter of time before machines can think like humans. Computers can already beat grand masters at chess! Other philosophers argue that humans are not just physical beings. They have "souls." Computers, on the other hand, are just machines that can process information.

HALF-HUMAN, HALF-MACHINE
The science fiction film "Terminator" imagines a world where humans and androids battle for control of Earth.

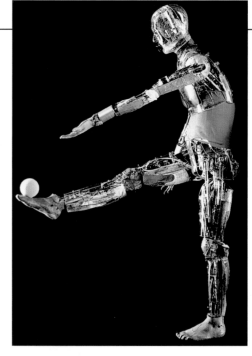

MECHANICAL MAN
Robots now do many jobs once done by humans. They can perform repetitive tasks cheaply and without getting bored.

ARE WE PLAYING GOD?

Ethics – the question of what is right and what is wrong – has always been of concern to philosophers. Advances in science are making possible what was once impossible. This has thrown new questions into focus. Today there are special committees to decide what limits to set in areas such as medicine, microbiology, and genetic engineering. Issues such as cloning (making an exact genetic replica of something) are hotly debated.

HELLO, DOLLY!
Dolly looks and behaves just like any other sheep. What makes Dolly unique is that she is a clone. It is now technically possible to clone a person.

"MIRACLES" OF SCIENCE
Rules governing procedures are vital now that human life can begin inside a lab.

WHAT RIGHT DO WE HAVE?

Our relationship with animals probably raises more ethical questions than any other. Do we humans have a right to use animals for our own ends? Some people maintain that we are superior because we have evolved beyond animal instinct. Others say that only humans have souls. This attitude was shared by philosophers in the past. Descartes thought that animals had no feelings (see pages 24–25).

But some animals display distinctly "human" traits: pets have performed acts of bravery, and some monkeys can even do math!

MORE INTELLIGENT THAN HUMANS?
Dolphins have much bigger brains than we do and have a sophisticated "language."

IS TIME TRAVEL POSSIBLE?

The idea of zipping around the galaxy in a time machine is another favorite science fiction theme. The nature of time is one of the fundamental questions in philosophy. Until Einstein came up with his theory of relativity, science had assumed that time and space were fixed backdrops to scientific inquiry. But Einstein proved that time slows down the faster an object moves. At 90 percent of the speed of light, a clock takes an hour to record 26 minutes. At the speed of light, time slows to zero. So what would happen if it were possible to travel faster than that? Is time a giant zipper that can move in only one direction? What if we could go back and alter the past...?

ACTION REPLAY
Superman's special powers allow him to fly so fast that he can reverse time.

ALBERT EINSTEIN'S THEORY
Einstein was just a humble office worker when he came up with his theory in 1905 at the age of 26. He was instantly famous.

SWEET DREAMS

People spend about a third of their lives asleep. It seems perfectly reasonable that the body needs to rest, but what about dreams?

Despite investigation, very little is actually known about why we dream. And dreaming isn't exclusive to humans, either – as anyone who has ever watched a sleeping pet is aware. So what is the mind playing at? In the world of dreams the laws of nature do not seem to apply. But dreams seem real at the time. They even cause physical reactions in the sleeper. No wonder so many philosophers think that beyond this life is another "higher" reality.

IN A WORLD OF HIS OWN
Scientists use electrodes to measure the brain patterns of sleeping people. This method can identify various sleep stages and detect when someone is dreaming.

WHAT'S IN THIS BOOK?

The first section of this book (pages 8–48) is a chronological journey through the history of Western philosophy, looking at the lives and the times of some of philosophy's greatest thinkers. Pronunciation guides will help you read their names.

None of these people existed in a vacuum. All philosophers are products of the times they were born in and the kinds of lives they led. Many have been influenced by the thoughts of those who lived before them. Looking at each philosopher in this context helps us to understand their ideas.

The second section of this book (pages 49–63) delves deeper into the work of these great philosophers. They are regrouped into schools of thought, which clearly show which philosophers shared similar ideas and who was influenced by whom. This section also allows us to take a look at some of the other important Western thinkers.

The glossary on page 63 explains various terms and expressions regularly used by philosophers.

THE EARLY GREEKS

THE HISTORY OF WESTERN PHILOSOPHY BEGAN IN ANCIENT GREECE. AT THIS TIME, GREECE was a collection of thriving and squabbling city-states. The ancient Greeks excelled in just about everything. A keen interest in the sciences gave some of them much food for thought. What made them "philosophers" was that they tried to explain the world scientifically. Before this, everything was explained by myths, legends, or the will of the gods.

ANCIENT GREECE
The culture that began in Greece in about 800 BC had expanded to include colonies all around the Mediterranean coast by the time of early philosophers.

Thales said that the world floated like a log on endless water.

He correctly predicted an eclipse of the Sun.

THALES
THAY-LEEZ

IT ALL STARTED WITH THALES. HE WAS THE FIRST PERSON TO BE GIVEN the label "wise." His home was Miletus, a busy port on the coast of Asia Minor (now Turkey). Traders passing through Miletus brought new ideas from all over the civilized world. Thales was an astronomer and an expert on managing water. He could navigate ships and reroute rivers. Knowing that water could be liquid, solid, and vapor, he wondered if that could explain how reality changed. Thales decided that water must be the basic ingredient of the universe.

Thales examined the world around him and recognized a vital life force that was present in everything. He said that "all things are full of gods."

ANAXIMANDER
AN-AX-UH-MAN-DER

ANAXIMANDER ALSO CAME FROM MILETUS. HE SHARED THALES' VIEW that there was a basic stuff that glued the universe together. But he didn't agree that it was anything as ordinary as water. He called this substance the "boundless" – something beyond the physical universe, but the source of everything in it. He thought that the world was shaped like a drum and surrounded by this boundless substance.

Anaximander also came up with the theory that people had evolved from fish. He reasoned that they must have evolved from something, because he could not see how a human baby could ever have survived if it had suddenly appeared in its present form.

Anaximander said people came from fish.

He drew a map of the known world.

He also invented a sundial.

ANAXIMENES
AN-AX-UH-MEEN-EEZ

ANAXIMENES WAS ANAXIMANDER'S PUPIL. HE LOOKED CAREFULLY AT THE natural world around him, then disagreed with his master. He believed the basic stuff that held everything together was air. He thought that all things were either thick air or thin air. As air got thicker it turned into wind, then clouds, then water, then mud and stones. Fire was just very thin air.

Anaximenes reasoned that air was the source of all life, because people have to breathe air to live. He also said people's souls were air. So his ideas about the universe explained both spiritual and material reality. He said, "As our soul, being air, holds us together and controls us, so does wind and air enclose the whole world."

Anaximenes thought the Earth was flat and rode on air.

He said the heavens moved around Earth like a hat on a head.

READ MORE ON PAGE 50

PYTHAGORAS
PUH-THAG-OR-US

THIS GREAT THINKER IS STILL FAMOUS TODAY FOR HIS THEOREM ABOUT triangles. In fact, Pythagoras was obsessed with numbers. He thought reality could be explained by mathematics. He also discovered a relationship between math and music and came up with a theory about the harmony of the universe.

Pythagoras was secretive about his work. He formed a society whose members followed a strict code. One rule was not to eat beans. They saw it as cannibalism, because a cut-open bean looks like the beginning of human life. This had tragic consequences. When chased by a hostile crowd, Pythagoras halted by a bean field. Rather than crush these "human beans," he met an untimely death.

Pythagoras said that reality is ten-sided.

He worked out a theory on triangles.

He banned the eating of beans.

HERACLITUS
HERR-UH-KLITE-US

LIKE THALES, HERACLITUS WAS INTERESTED IN CHANGE. IN FACT, HE saw that nothing in the world stayed the same from one minute to the next. This is what he meant when he said that you can never step into the same river twice. Heraclitus searched for a basic substance to explain this change, and he decided it must be fire. Fire has a stable appearance, yet it changes everything it touches. His saw the world as being in a constant state of creation and destruction. He also recognized a logic behind everything – a kind of cosmic balance. He understood that without winter there could be no spring, and without bad there would be no yardstick for good.

Heraclitus said the basic substance of the universe is fire.

He said that no one can step in the same river twice.

PARMENIDES
PAR-MEN-UH-DEEZ

PARMENIDES DECIDED THAT WHAT HIS SENSES TOLD HIM DIDN'T MAKE ANY sense. Although his eyes told him that everything changes, his reason told him that this was an illusion. If everything changes, how did the world begin in the first place? He decided that the world must have always existed because a *nothing* could not suddenly change into a *something*. He reasoned that the world would exist forever, because a *something* couldn't change into a *nothing*.

Parmenides believed that reality could be understood only by thought. He imagined reality as an invisible, unchanging ball. He also said that the origin of all apparent difference is darkness and light.

Parmenides did not think reality could be seen.

He said reality was a huge ball-shaped thing, invisible to the senses.

EMPEDOCLES
EM-PED-UH-KLEEZ

EMPEDOCLES CAME FROM SICILY. HE WAS DIFFERENT FROM THE EARLY Greeks before him, because he disagreed that there was one basic ingredient to the universe. He said reality boiled down to the simplest parts of the four elements (fire, air, earth, and water). All change could be explained by the coming together and falling apart of these elements. He said that there are two basic forces in nature that cause this – love and strife. Love brings things together and strife tears them apart. This idea explained both how things can change and how the world remains the same.

His theory on evolution was that only the strong survived. Sadly, he didn't survive a jump into Mount Etna.

Empedocles wrote in rhyme most of the time.

He dived into a volcano to prove he was a god and burned to a crisp.

11

READ MORE ON PAGES 50, 54, 62

SOCRATES

Socrates loved city life, saying that he could learn nothing from trees in the country.

He listened to an inner voice, which stopped him from doing things for selfish reasons.

He saw himself as a horsefly, stinging Athens to life.

Athens' Parthenon was dedicated to Athena, goddess of wisdom.

Socrates fought in Athens' wars with Sparta.

His words were recorded by Plato, his most famous pupil.

Sophists were wise men who charged for their knowledge.

Socrates' wife was annoyed that he would not teach for money.

He went barefoot, even in winter.

Before he died, he paid off a debt with a chicken.

He protested in political matters and made some powerful enemies.

SOCRATES WAS A FAMILIAR FIGURE IN ATHENS. SHABBILY DRESSED AND ALWAYS BAREFOOT, HE spent his days discussing everything under the sun with all and sundry. He was soon regarded as the wisest man in Athens, even though the city was full of philosophers who charged money for teaching. This flattery did not impress Socrates. He said, "The only thing I know is that I know nothing." He also said:

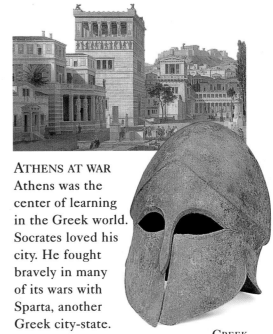

ATHENS AT WAR
Athens was the center of learning in the Greek world. Socrates loved his city. He fought bravely in many of its wars with Sparta, another Greek city-state.

GREEK SOLDIER'S HELMET

"IGNORANCE IS THE ONLY EVIL"

Socrates believed that happiness came from leading a good life. What is good and what is bad? This was the big question. Socrates thought he might find out if he talked to enough people. The more questions he asked, the more he would know, and knowledge was the one thing he was sure was good. But his challenging questions got him into trouble. Some of Athens' leading political figures did not take kindly to having their opinions reduced to shreds.

Socrates was arrested and accused of corrupting young minds and worshipping false gods. He was found guilty on both charges and sentenced to death by drinking poisonous hemlock. His accusers expected him to beg for his life. Their real intention was to take this colorful character down a peg or two. Under Athenian law, Socrates had the chance to suggest a different punishment. But he refused to grovel. Instead, he proposed that the city should give him one free meal a day and erect a statue of himself in the marketplace. The court was not amused and ordered the death sentence to be carried out.

The old philosopher was honest (and penniless) to the end. Rather than die owing money, he paid off his final debt with a chicken.

HEMLOCK
This poisonous plant is common throughout Europe. It causes paralysis and death. In Greece it was administered as a capital punishment.

THE DEATH OF SOCRATES
Socrates drank the hemlock and died comforting his grieving friends.

READ MORE ON PAGE 49

PLATO

Plato believed in an unseen world where there existed the perfect models of all things on the Earth.

Our world is a world of shadows, mere reflections of an ideal world.

People are like trapped prisoners who only ever see shadows. They mistake these shadows for what is real.

Plato wrote down his ideas as conversations.

Plato founded the first university.

Plato's ideal society would be ruled by philosophers.

Courageous soldiers would help to keep order.

Ordinary folk would have a fair and stable government.

Plato believed in educating women.

He believed in an eternal soul that came from the ideal world.

PLATO WAS BORN INTO THE ARISTOCRACY OF ATHENS,

AND HE COULD VERY EASILY HAVE RISEN to a position of power. But what he saw of the cut-throat, rough-and-tumble of politics disgusted him. Plato knew that a good government would never have murdered a good man like Socrates. The tragic death of his friend and teacher spurred Plato to do something that would change things. He believed that good leaders weren't born, they had the right education. So he opened his own school. From then on, his teachings focused on one big question:

PLATO'S ACADEMY
The Academy lay in pretty countryside near Athens. Students studied science, gymnastics, and philosophy. Plato dedicated his university to the Muses, goddesses of music and education.

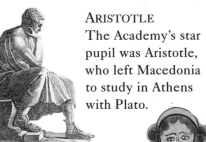

THE MUSES

"IS THERE A PERFECT WORLD?"

Socrates never wrote down his thoughts. Plato wanted to make sure that the great thinker was never forgotten, and so he recorded Socrates' ideas. He did this in the form of discussions between two people, often making Socrates the main voice. Plato was a gifted writer, and these dialogues were a hit with his audience. So he continued writing them, even after he started developing his own ideas. This makes it hard to be certain where Socrates' ideas ended and Plato's began.

Socrates wanted to find unchanging truths about abstract things like goodness and justice. Plato went a step further. He thought there were unchanging truths behind all things. For example, there are many breeds of horses, but there is a definite "horseness" about them all. Plato imagined another world where there is a perfect and eternal model for everything ("horseness," "dogness," "catness," courage, justice – absolutely everything). He said that the Earth is just a world of fleeting shadows. Plato saw it as a philosopher's job to open people's eyes to this and to help them strive toward perfection.

ARISTOTLE
The Academy's star pupil was Aristotle, who left Macedonia to study in Athens with Plato.

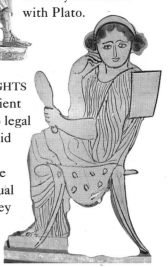

WOMEN'S RIGHTS
Women in ancient Greece had no legal rights. Plato said that men and women had the same intellectual powers and they should receive the same education.

READ MORE ON PAGE 51

ARISTOTLE

Aristotle tutored the young Alexander the Great.

He saw that every acorn has the potential to grow into an oak tree.

Aristotle branded women second-class citizens, unfit for any legal or political rights.

He opened his own school in Athens called the Lyceum.

Aristotle came to Athens to study at Plato's Academy.

He found that he could sort everything on Earth into animal, vegetable, and mineral.

Aristotle excelled at marine biology and identified 500 different species of sea life.

Aristotle liked to walk and talk as he taught his students.

Aristotle studied with Plato for twenty years, and many of Plato's ideas can be seen in his work. However, Aristotle thought that Plato's unseen world of perfect forms was perfect nonsense. He was altogether more down to earth than Plato. The natural world fascinated Aristotle, and he was often seen down on all fours, peering at plants or watching the antics of creepy-crawlies. He declared:

TEACHING ALEXANDER THE GREAT
Aristotle took a break from studying to go to Macedonia as tutor to the king's son. The young prince grew up to conquer all the known world.

ALEXANDER IN BATTLE

"THERE IS SOMETHING MARVELOUS IN ALL NATURAL THINGS"

After Plato's death, Aristotle opened his own school, the Lyceum, where Plato's philosophy was studied, as well as criticized. Aristotle believed that Plato's perfect forms were part of life, not apart from it.

Studying nature convinced him that everything was striving toward its own unique form of perfection. He knew that all acorns were potential oak trees, even though many landed on barren soil. He also knew that a duck's egg would never hatch into an eagle.

Aristotle was a great organizer. He looked at the chaotic jumble of creation and tried to sort it into neat piles. His aim was to categorize all areas of human knowledge. He sifted through everything, even separating language into ten basic word-types.

But he did make errors, and pigeonholing women as "unfinished men" was a big one. With no such thing as microbiology to prove otherwise, he said only men carried human "seed." This put women on a par with soil and deeply harmed their credibility centuries later.

ARISTOTLE AND THE CHURCH
In the Middle Ages much of Aristotle's thinking was accepted by the Church. Even his view that women were inferior to men seemed to fit in with the Bible story of Eve's creation from Adam's rib.

READ MORE ON PAGE 53

EPICURUS AND ZENO

Epicurus, a Greek, founded his school in a garden near Athens.

Epicurus's followers were called "garden philosophers."

Zeno, a Greek, founded the Stoics in the center of Athens.

Stoics got their name because Zeno taught from a porch (stoa in Greek).

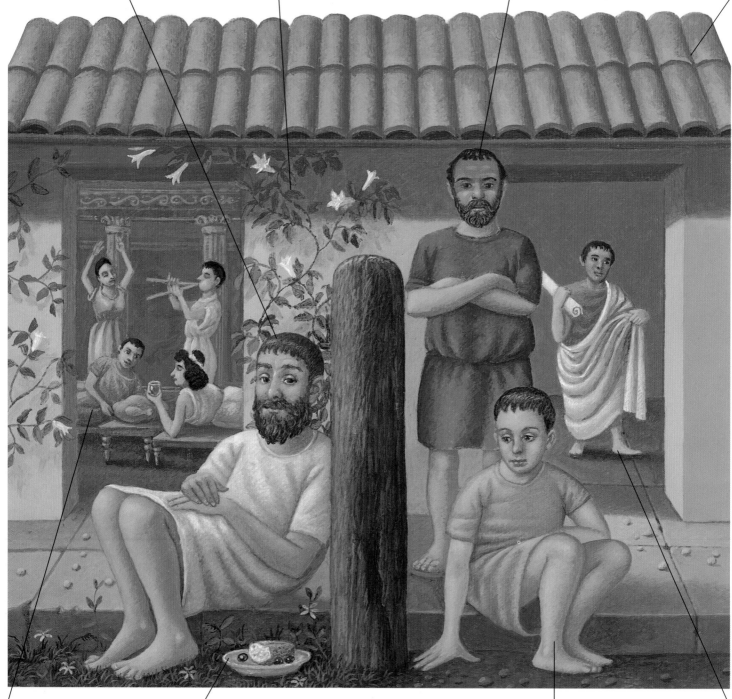

In Roman times many Epicureans took the seeking of pleasure to extremes.

Simple food, good friends, and avoiding pain were Epicurus's idea of pleasure.

Children were important to the Stoics because the future was part of a divine plan.

Roman Stoics tried to be virtuous and would not be led by emotions.

IN ABOUT 300 BC, ZENO AND EPICURUS EACH FOUNDED A SCHOOL OF PHILOSOPHY IN ATHENS. Both schools had roots in the quest of Socrates – how to lead a good life. However, Zeno's followers (the Stoics) were very different from the Epicureans. Stoics believed that they were part of a divine plan and that whatever happened was meant to be. Epicureans thought human existence was just a random grouping of atoms that fell apart after death. Their motto was "don't worry, be happy." Above the entrance to their school were the words:

"PLEASURE IS THE HIGHEST GOOD"

Epicurus's idea of pleasure was to enjoy the simple things in life. Time to relax was at the top of the list. He preferred to eat a simple meal with friends rather than risk a stomachache at a lavish banquet. In fact, he urged followers to think twice before pursuing any pleasure that might cause pain. Even falling in love can end in a broken heart.

To the Stoics, a good life meant a virtuous one. They refused to be ruled by their feelings, because emotions just got in the way of good judgment. Their philosophy was to put up with their lot in life. Stoics didn't try to fight fate. Their motto was "go with the flow." Wanting what they couldn't have could only bring unhappiness. They decided to want whatever they got – this way they could never feel let down.

Greece became part of the Roman Empire some 150 years after Zeno and Epicurus founded their schools. The Romans adopted and adapted these two philosophies – along with many other things Greek.

Stoicism appealed to all classes of society – from slave to emperor. But Roman Epicureans gave the school a bad name. Pleasure-seeking became an excuse for satisfying every desire and living for the moment.

DIOGENES THE CYNIC MEETS HIS KING
Early Stoics were similar to the Cynics, who had no regard for authority. One story recounts a chance meeting between Diogenes and Alexander the Great, ruler of all Greece. The king was upset by Diogenes' seeming poverty and asked if he could do anything. "Yes, move!" said the Cynic, "You're blocking my sun!"

SENECA (4 BC–AD 65)
This Roman Stoic was a lawyer and a poet. He was also tutor to the mad emperor Nero. Seneca took his own life rather than be a party to Nero's cruel deeds.

MARCUS AURELIUS (AD 120–180)
The Roman emperor Marcus Aurelius tried to live the Stoic ideal of a virtuous life. He avoided extravagance and put the empire's needs above his own.

READ MORE ON PAGES 50, 51

HYPATIA

Hypatia taught a close circle of students, who all were male and aristocratic.

The head of the Christian church in Alexandria banished all the Jews from the city.

The Christians destroyed temples and statues dedicated to pagan religions.

The lighthouse at Alexandria was one of the Seven Wonders of the World.

Hypatia was a gifted astronomer.

Hypatia helped students get in touch with their spiritual nature, or the "eye within."

She always rode around the city in a chariot.

She dressed simply, wearing the white cloak of a philosopher.

Her enemies incited the Christians to drag her from her chariot and murder her.

HYPATIA WAS AN ASTRONOMER AND MATHEMATICIAN AS

WELL AS A PHILOSOPHER. SHE WAS AN Egyptian of Greek descent, renowned for her great beauty. Hypatia's philosophy was also her religion. She believed in a divine being called "the One" – the ultimate source of all reality. Her aim was to get closer to "the One," and she shared her methods with a select circle of students. She taught them to break free from the world of matter by seeking the divine part of human nature, or the soul. She called it:

"THE EYE BURIED WITHIN US"

At this time women were not considered equal. But to her students, all of whom were male, Hypatia was above womanhood. She demanded complete dedication and wouldn't put up with any nonsense. When one student got distracted from his path toward "the One" by falling in love with her, Hypatia dangled a soiled item of her personal clothing in front of him and said, "This is me. This is what you love!" He was a model pupil from then on. Hypatia's point was that earthly beauty is an illusion. True beauty existed only in "the One."

Hypatia lived in Alexandria, which was the third largest city in the Roman Empire. It was a center of learning, and a melting pot of cultures. In her day, there was a lot of strife between Christians, Jews, and pagans. Hypatia tried to stay out of the battles. The whole city respected her wisdom, and the Roman governor often asked her advice on city affairs. This sealed her fate. The governor was locked in a bitter power struggle with the local head of the Christian church, who saw Hypatia as a threat. Rumors spread that she practiced black magic, and Hypatia was blamed for all the city's woes. One day, as she was riding home, a group of outraged Christians dragged her from her chariot and cut her to pieces with sharpened seashells.

ALEXANDRIA Alexander the Great conquered Egypt in 332 BC and built a new capital. Alexandria stands where the Nile River flows into the Mediterranean Sea.

PLOTINUS (AD 204–270) Hypatia was probably influenced by Plotinus. They were both Neoplatonists, who adopted Plato's idea of a perfect spirit. Plotinus thought that a union of soul, mind, and "the One" glued the world together.

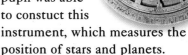

ASTROLABE As a result of Hypatia's teaching, a pupil was able to constuct this instrument, which measures the position of stars and planets.

EMPEROR CONSTANTINE In AD 312 the pagan emperor Constantine became a Christian. Soon after this, Christianity became the official religion of the Roman Empire.

READ MORE ON PAGE 52

AQUINAS

Aquinas combined the philosophy of Aristotle with the Christian religion.

Thomas Aquinas was the seventh son of an Italian count.

When Aquinas ran away to join the Dominican friars, his brothers kidnapped him and took him home.

Aquinas was educated in a monastery, like many children during the Middle Ages.

SUMMA CONTRA GENTILES

SUMMA THEOLOGIAE

Aquinas said all living things have souls. Plant souls ensure growth.

Animals have souls capable of feeling.

People's souls have the ability to reason.

Angels are between human beings and God.

Aquinas grew so fat he had to have a special niche cut into his table.

He was made a saint as a result of his work.

A 13TH-CENTURY FRIAR CALLED THOMAS AQUINAS TRIED TO SHOW THAT PHILOSOPHY AND religion need not be at loggerheads. He said that faith and reason were often two paths to the same end. Through reason, the Greek philosopher Aristotle had identified an "unmoved mover," a supreme being whose existence at the beginning of time set the universe in motion. To Aquinas, this harmonized with the Christians' faith in God, who created all things. He argued that without God there could be no universe:

BENEDICTINES Aquinas was taught by Benedictine monks, and his family wanted him to join this order.

PHILOSOPHER AVERROES (1126–1198) In the Dark Ages Greek philosophy was kept alive by the Arab world. Averroes revered Aristotle, calling him a prophet. Aquinas read translations of Arab texts.

"TO TAKE AWAY THE CAUSE IS TO TAKE AWAY THE EFFECT"

Aquinas was the son of an Italian nobleman. At the age of 19 he ran away from home to join Dominican friars in France. His brothers promptly brought him back and kept him holed up in the family castle for a year, trying to bring him to his senses. But nothing would discourage him, and eventually his family relented.

Dominican friars were intellectuals, trained to answer questions challenging Christianity. After hundreds of years in obscurity, Greek philosophy was once again being studied. Aquinas absorbed many of Aristotle's ideas and used them as a platform for his own thinking. His aim was to prove God's existence through reason (the tool of the philosopher). The result was two massive books in which he managed to weld the philosophy of Aristotle to Christian belief.

After experiencing some kind of divine vision, Aquinas stopped writing, saying words were "mere straw." Two years later, a bump on the head caused a decline in health. He spent his last days in an Italian monastery, where he was discovered dead in the lavatory. After his death, Aquinas's work became the approved philosophy of the Church and earned him a place with the saints.

DOMINICAN FRIARS The Dominicans were founded in 1206 by Saint Dominic to oppose a religious group in France. They were noted preachers, teachers, and missionaries.

The order's headquarters are now in Rome. A Dominican friar traditionally holds the post of chief advisor to the Pope.

AQUINAS JOINS THE DOMINICANS

READ MORE ON PAGE 54

DESCARTES

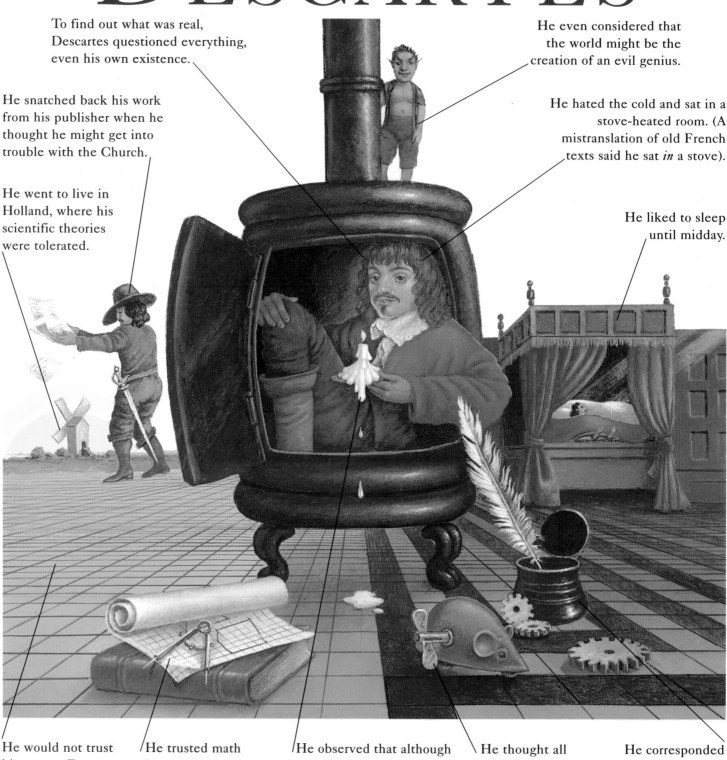

To find out what was real, Descartes questioned everything, even his own existence.

He snatched back his work from his publisher when he thought he might get into trouble with the Church.

He went to live in Holland, where his scientific theories were tolerated.

He even considered that the world might be the creation of an evil genius.

He hated the cold and sat in a stove-heated room. (A mistranslation of old French texts said he sat *in* a stove).

He liked to sleep until midday.

He would not trust his senses. For example, distance can distort things.

He trusted math because, asleep or awake, two plus three always equals five.

He observed that although wax changes in every way when it melts, his mind told him it was still wax.

He thought all animals were mindless robots.

He corresponded with the queen of Sweden, who invited him to tutor her.

FRENCHMAN DESCARTES TURNED PHILOSOPHY ON ITS

HEAD AND STARTED AGAIN. FIRST, HE had to find out what he knew for certain. He did this by doubting everything. Could he believe what he saw with his eyes, when big things looked small in the distance? How did he know that he really existed? Maybe he was dreaming. Having to doubt his own existence almost drove Descartes mad. Luckily, he came up with the answer:

MATHEMATICIAN
Descartes was brilliant at math. He broke new ground in geometry.

PHILOSOPHER TO A QUEEN
This 17th-century painting shows Descartes demonstrating his theories to Queen Christina of Sweden.

"I THINK, THEREFORE I AM"

Awake or dreaming, Descartes was in no doubt at all that he was thinking. And if he could think, then *he must exist.* He decided that reality is made up of two separate things – mind and body.

Descartes spent the rest of his life trying to figure out how minds and bodies work together. He was a scientist at heart, but at the time the Church was persecuting Galileo and other scientists for their scientific theories. So Descartes moved to Holland, where they were more relaxed about new ideas. Here, there was great interest in mechanical objects like clocks. Descartes came to the conclusion that the body is like a machine. But he found it tricky explaining how the mind is able to connect to the body. After much head-scratching, he finally announced that the meeting point is a small gland in the brain.

The queen of Sweden was very interested in his theories and invited him to go there to teach her. But Sweden's icy climate and the fact that the queen could only see him for early morning lessons did not agree with Descartes, whose pet peeves were cold weather and getting up early. The combination of these two things had a bad affect on his health. A cold turned to pneumonia, and he died.

GALILEO'S TELESCOPE
This invention confirmed that the Earth orbited the Sun. The Church taught that the Earth was the center of the universe, but Descartes agreed with Galileo.

CHURCH INQUISITION
Galileo was brought to trial and found guilty of heresy. He was imprisoned for life. Descartes was careful that his own work did not upset the Church.

READ MORE ON PAGE 55

SPINOZA

Spinoza's Jewish parents came to Amsterdam to escape persecution.

Spinoza said that God and all of the natural universe were one substance.

He was expelled from the Jewish community because of his beliefs.

Spinoza was an expert in optics. He made a meager living grinding lenses.

Like Descartes, he used geometric formulas to try to find out the truth about the universe.

He refused to dedicate a book to Louis XIV in return for a royal pension.

He was attacked by a knife-wielding assassin on the synagogue steps.

BY ALL ACCOUNTS SPINOZA WAS A KIND, GENTLE, AND CONSIDERATE MAN. HE WAS ALSO A MAN of principle. He refused a university post because he did not wish to compromise his ideals, and he would not take money for his genius, preferring to earn his living as a humble lens grinder. Unlike many of the great thinkers, Spinoza tried to live according to his philosophy. As a result he was hated by almost everyone. However, he survived expulsion from his religion, rejection by his family, and an attempt on his life to say:

"THERE CANNOT BE TOO MUCH JOY"

JOHN CALVIN (1509–1564)
Calvinism was Holland's state religion. Spinoza admired the simple lifestyle of the Collegiants, another Protestant sect, and changed his name to Benedict.

WORKING WITH LENSES
Spinoza was a friend of the astronomer Christian Huygens, the founder of modern optics.

17TH-CENTURY OPTICAL MICROSCOPE

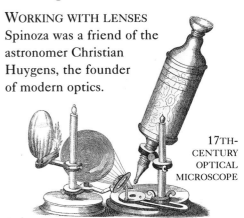

Spinoza was a Dutch Jew of Spanish descent, whose parents had come to Amsterdam to escape persecution from the Catholic Church. As a youth, he studied the Jewish philosophers, but the most abiding influence on his thinking was Descartes.

Like Descartes, Spinoza believed that reason was how people make sense of the world. But whereas Descartes had said that the universe is made up of two things – mind and matter, Spinoza said that there is only one substance – God. God and the universe and everything in it are one and the same. To make matters worse, Spinoza said that people have no special place in the cosmos. The Jews were especially indignant about this. Their faith taught them that they were God's chosen people. Spinoza was hauled in front of the synagogue elders and thrown out of the flock. His beliefs so outraged the Jewish community that an attempt was made on his life. He kept the knife-slashed cloak as a memento.

Spinoza stayed true to his principles all his life and, although he made enemies, many people admired his integrity. At age 45, he died of consumption, made worse by glass dust from his lens-grinding.

PLIGHT OF THE JEWS
Jews in 16th-century Spain were forced to become Catholics or flee the country. Many went to Amsterdam.

AMSTERDAM'S FIRST SYNAGOGUE
In 1598 the Jews were given permission to build a synagogue. Holland's Jews were anxious to safeguard their heritage. Spinoza's beliefs were seen as a threat.

READ MORE ON PAGE 56

LOCKE

When Locke was a boy, there was a civil war between the King and the parliament. The King's supporters lost the war.

He wrote romantic letters to his many lady friends, but he never married.

Locke was a lecturer at Oxford University.

Locke is the only philosopher to have become a minister of government.

Locke studied medicine part-time and became well qualified.

Agents of the King spied on Locke.

His father was an inspector of sewers.

Locke's friend Isaac Newton discovered gravity.

Locke operated on the Lord Chancellor's diseased liver, in which he placed a silver tap.

ENGLISHMAN JOHN LOCKE STARTED A NEW VOGUE IN THINKING. HE LIKED RENÉ DESCARTES'S method of clearing the slate to find out how people got to know things. But human reason wasn't the answer that Locke came up with. He said that all knowledge begins with what comes to the mind through the senses. Only then can people begin to organize this information through reason. He said that no one knows anything at birth.

KING CHARLES I'S EXECUTION
Locke lived through a civil war, caused by the King's belief in a God-given right to rule. The King was put to death.

OLIVER CROMWELL
Cromwell, the rebel leader, became Lord Protector of England. After 11 years of strict Puritan rule, Charles II was crowned king.

"THE MIND IS A BLANK PIECE OF PAPER"

Locke grew up during England's civil war. His father fought for parliament against the King. The local member of parliament thanked him by sending young John to an exclusive school. This lucky quirk of fate set Locke on the road to a glittering future. The same politician, however, appointed Locke's father local inspector of sewers.

Locke became interested in medicine at Oxford University. He also rubbed shoulders with many famous people. The most powerful was Lord Shaftesbury, who made Locke his personal secretary and doctor. When an abscessed liver threatened to kill Shaftesbury, Locke drained it with a silver tap. Shaftesbury wore it for the rest of his life.

Shaftesbury rose to be Lord Chancellor, and he made Locke a government minister. But Shaftesbury's intrigues got them both into trouble with Charles II, the newly reinstated king. Locke was a careful man, however. He wrote his notes in code and crossed out names and places. He even used invisible ink for erotic parts of the long, flowery letters he sent his lady friends. The King's spies reported that Locke lived "a very cunning and unintelligible life."

The dog-eat-dog political arena convinced Locke of the need for tolerance. He said that all people had these basic rights: the right to life, to freedom, to own property, and to revolt against unjust rule.

LOCKE'S LEGACY
The American Constitution embodies Locke's political ideas. Here George Washington, the first president, accepts the signed Constitution (1787).

SLAVE TRADE
Locke believed that people were equal because nature made them free. It is ironic that, as a minister, he was in charge of England's lucrative slave trade.

SLAVE'S NECK COLLAR

READ MORE ON PAGE 57

HUME

Hume went to Edinburgh University at 12 to study law, but he found it boring.

The university later rejected Hume as a lecturer because he questioned God's existence.

Hume was welcomed in France, where his writing made him a huge success.

In France he became friends with the philosopher Rousseau, but they later fought.

He worked in the British embassy in Paris for three years.

Hume wasn't a stylish dresser, but people were attracted by his charm.

Hume said that people expect a falling glass to break.

Hume questioned that one thing (broken glass) is caused by another (falling glass).

He made a lot of money from book sales.

THE SCOTTISH THINKER DAVID HUME WANTED TO BRING PHILOSOPHY TO ITS SENSES. HE scoffed at so-called human reason. Like John Locke, Hume believe that what people knew of the world began with the senses. He set out to discover whether there was any real proof of those things that people took for granted. His conclusions pulled the rug out from under both science and religion. Hume's questioning of God's existence might have cost him his life a century or so earlier. It still caused a public scandal. This may be why he said:

ADAM SMITH
The economist Adam Smith was Hume's closest friend. They shared similar views, such as a belief that free trade between nations is of mutual benefit.

EDINBURGH IN 1763
Calton Hill, where Hume was buried, overlooks his beloved home city.

"ERRORS IN RELIGION ARE DANGEROUS, THOSE IN PHILOSOPHY ONLY RIDICULOUS"

Hume's family were Scottish gentry. His mother wanted him to be a lawyer, but he was more interested in philosophy. By 27 he had gathered his thoughts together, and they were published under the title *A Treatise of Human Nature*. Hume made no secret of the fact that his ultimate ambition was literary fame and fortune. And so he was somewhat upset when his book went unnoticed. It was history, not philosophy, that brought him success. Hume's *History of England* was a best-seller. When the *Treatise* was revised and published ten years later under a new title, it got the attention Hume knew it deserved.

Hume said all knowledge boiled down to two sources – impressions and ideas. Impressions are direct experiences, whereas ideas are just memories of impressions. The brain can sort and combine ideas into complex creations that do not exist in reality. For example, the idea of mermaid combines the impressions "fish" and "woman". Ideas such as heaven and hell exist only in the imagination until proved to be real. He also challenged accepted scientific laws, such as gravity and cause-and-effect. His view was that they are accepted in the same way that someone who has only ever seen brown cows thinks all cows are brown.

ALBERT EINSTEIN (1879–1955)
Einstein named Hume as a major influence when he came up with his theory of relativity. Einstein's theory shocked scientists because it stated that time and space are not fixed things.

READ MORE ON PAGE 57

KANT

People could set their watches by Kant's daily walk.

One day he stayed in to read a book, and people were late all over town.

Kant was a professor of philosophy at Königsberg University.

He said that reason distinguished right from wrong. If people went around killing each other, no one would be left.

Kant spent most of his time writing and studying. His early work was about science.

His theory on the solar system stated that most planets are inhabited.

Kant found the novel *Emile* by Rousseau food for thought.

Kant said that a person's view of reality is distorted by how the mind works.

IMMANUEL KANT WAS A MAN OF HABIT, LIVING HIS LIFE TO A PRECISE ROUTINE. TOWNSFOLK USED to set their watches by his afternoon walk, since he followed the same route at the same time every day. He led a strangely uneventful life. He never married, never fell ill, and never even traveled far from his home town of Königsberg in east Prussia. But Immanuel Kant was a great thinker. When he died at the age of 80, these words were inscribed on his tombstone:

DAVID HUME This Scottish philosopher made Kant rethink his belief that all knowledge was based on reason.

ROUSSEAU The Swiss writer Jean-Jacques Rousseau was also a philosopher. He believed that people were naturally good; only civilization made them bad. His novel *Emile* prompted Kant's views on the nature of morals.

"TWO THINGS FILL MY MIND WITH EVER-INCREASING WONDER AND AWE, THE STARRY HEAVENS ABOVE ME AND THE MORAL LAW WITHIN ME"

At the time when Napoleon was on the march through Europe, philosophy was at a stalemate. There were two opposing schools of thought. One said that all knowledge came from experience. The other said that human reason made sense of the world. Kant tried to bring the two together. He set about this by exploring how the human mind works and what reality actually is.

The upshot was called a revolution in thinking. But because of his tedious and unfathomable writing style, it took a little while for his brilliance to be recognized.

According to Kant, no one can say for certain what reality is, only what it appears to be to them. This is because the human mind molds reality into a form that makes sense to it. Kant called space and time "irremovable goggles." They weren't "things" to be found out in the world, they were part of the mind's structuring system.

Kant said it was a moral necessity to believe in God, even though it was beyond the ability of human reason to prove God's existence. He argued that people were governed by a universal moral law.

LOUIS XVI'S EXECUTION

FRENCH REVOLUTION News of the French Revolution was one of only two times Kant did not take his daily walk. To Kant, the event symbolized freedom of action.

MARTIN LUTHER Kant was a strict follower of Martin Luther, who preached that faith in God was more important than proof of God's existence.

33

READ MORE ON PAGE 58

HEGEL

Hegel said that people will eventually know everything in the process of history.

Hegel planted a "liberty tree" to celebrate the French Revolution.

Hegel's landlord evicted him for having an affair with his wife.

He worked for a pro-Napoleon newspaper.

He said world leaders like Julius Caesar change the course of history.

He finished his first major work on the day Napoleon took over the city.

He thought Napoleon was the best thing since sliced bread.

When Hegel wasn't busy writing long, obscure books, he liked a game of cards.

He lectured at the new University of Berlin.

Students came from far and wide to hear his long-winded lectures.

HEGEL WAS NOT A MODEST MAN. HE CLAIMED THAT HE UNDERSTOOD ALL OF PHILOSOPHY AND

history. Like Spinoza, he thought that God and the universe were inseparable. It is difficult to describe Hegel's philosophy simply, because it isn't simple. It is a huge, all-embracing system that moves through history like a giant snowball, gathering the best from every era, forever expanding human knowledge. Eventually it will arrive at the absolute truth – God. Hegel disagreed with Kant, who said it was beyond human reason to understand God. He said:

"ALL KNOWLEDGE IS HUMAN KNOWLEDGE"

VON SCHELLING
Fellow philosopher Schelling accused Hegel of stealing his ideas. This ended their long friendship, which began when they were both students.

A REVOLUTION IN FRANCE
In 1789 the starving lower classes rose up against the aristocracy, sending shock waves across Europe. Hegel welcomed this as a new age of freedom.

The basis of Hegel's system is a continuing process of argument, which goes on and on until it arrives at the ultimate revelation. He saw history as humanity's path to self-discovery, and he singled out "world spirits," such as Julius Caesar, who brought in each new era.

Hegel was born in Stuttgart. At this time, Germany was a loose collection of states, which were run on the feudal system of serf and master. When Hegel was 36 and a professor, Napoleon conquered Germany. Hegel saw him as the new "world spirit," even though the university was closed and he had to work on a newspaper for a year.

Hegel's plodding style earned him the title "the old man" – even as a young one. His lectures could never be described as scintillating. Nevertheless his reputation spread far and wide, and many came to listen to him. They were happy to suffer his lumbering, humorless delivery just to be able to bathe in his genius. But Hegel wasn't a stuffed shirt with the ladies. In fact, he was thrown out of his lodgings for dallying with his landlord's wife. In his forties he settled down with a wife half his age. They had two children and lived happily until Hegel fell ill with cholera. He died at 61 at the height of his fame.

KARL MARX
Hegel's philosophy spawned many groups of followers, even years after his death. Karl Marx adopted some of Hegel's ideas as a basis for a new political system known as Marxism.

KARL MARX AT AGE 57

READ MORE ON PAGE 52

NIETZSCHE

Nietzsche proposed that life eternally repeats itself, and that each person lives the same life again and again.

His father was a Lutheran preacher.

Nietzsche grew up to be strongly critical of Christianity.

He became a professor at the age of 24.

Nietzsche wrote about a prophet who announced "God is dead."

Nietzsche's "superman" combined strength, intellect, and creativity.

He thought that the ancient Greeks had achieved the right balance between order and passion.

Nietzsche finally went insane and spent his last years in the care of his sister.

The main theme of his books is that individuals should try to achieve their full potential.

The composer Richard Wagner became a close friend, but they later fought.

For ten years Nietzsche dropped out of society and lived in the Alps.

His writing style left his work open to interpretation by extremist groups.

WHEN NIETZSCHE WAS A BOY HE WAS CALLED "THE LITTLE PASTOR." HE EXPECTED TO BE A clergyman like his father, but in college he began to question his upbringing. He decided that Christianity robbed people of the will to excel. His ideal was the artistic warrior hero of ancient Greece. In his eyes, people were not created equal. There were men, and there were supermen. Nietzsche thought that these "higher" beings were the key to the future. He thought the Christian era had had its day. That was the message behind his statement:

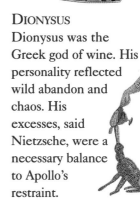

APOLLO
Nietzsche believed the Greek gods Apollo and Dionysus embodied the two sides of human nature. Sun god Apollo stood for order and harmony.

DIONYSUS
Dionysus was the Greek god of wine. His personality reflected wild abandon and chaos. His excesses, said Nietzsche, were a necessary balance to Apollo's restraint.

"GOD IS DEAD"

Nietzsche blamed cultural decay on the belief that being poor and submissive was good, but being rich and masterful was wicked. His studies taught him that different societies prized different values.

He said Plato had started the decay by coming up with the idea of another reality behind this one. Fear of an eternal hell made people repress their natural passions, abilities, and differences. Nietzsche preferred the idea of "eternal recurrence," meaning that this life is the only reality, but that it will be repeated forever. He urged people to live life as a work of art. Nietzsche's "superman" was a lover of life and would welcome the chance to repeat it in every detail.

Nietzsche's own life was dogged by illness, first physical, then mental. The cracks began to show in his autobiography with chapters such as "Why I am so clever" and "Why I write such good books."

Nietzsche's name is tainted by those who took his ideas and used them for their own ends. For the last ten years of his life he was clinically insane and was cared for by his sister, who edited his work to fit in with her own narrow views. Years after Nietzsche's death, she saw Hitler as the prototype "superman." History tells the rest.

RICHARD WAGNER
Nietzsche idolized Wagner's great talent. But he later became disillusioned with the flamboyant composer, who became an anti-Jewish nationalist and whose extravagance broke the Bavarian bank.

WAGNER WITH HIS WIFE COSIMA

READ MORE ON PAGE 62

HUSSERL

Husserl studied math before he got interested in philosophy.

He thought philosophy could be conducted along the lines of a scientific experiment.

Husserl's philosophy was about the "here" and "now."

He tried to step back from himself to observe consciousness working.

His wife was behind him in everything he did.

Descartes's idea of doubting everything was a big ingredient of Husserl's philosophy.

Kant's idea that reality was colored by people's view of the world was another big ingredient.

He said that clocks could tell you nothing about the real nature of time.

SOME SAY 20TH-CENTURY PHILOSOPHY BEGAN WITH EDMUND HUSSERL. HE INVENTED A NEW way of looking at the world. He called it "phenomenology," meaning "how things appear." Husserl wanted to find a foolproof method of measuring reality. Like Descartes, he believed that consciousness is the key. And like Kant, he understood that consciousness is shaped by how the mind works. Husserl also realized something else about consciousness – it doesn't exist in a vacuum. It is impossible to think nothing. He observed:

FRANZ BRENTANO
Husserl studied under Brentano, a psychologist and ex-priest. Brentano's ideas were pioneering and influenced Husserl's work.

FREIBURG UNIVERSITY, GERMANY
Husserl taught for many years at Freiburg. But because of his Jewish parentage, he was excluded after Hitler rose to power.

"ALL CONSCIOUSNESS IS CONSCIOUSNESS OF SOMETHING"

Husserl spent 40 years of his life as a philosophy professor. Before this he was already highly qualified in mathematics and astronomy – subjects that nurtured a desire to apply scientific method to philosophy.

Husserl wanted to strip consciousness down to its essence to reveal how it shaped reality. Rather than doubting everything, like Descartes, Husserl pushed to one side (or "bracketed," as he called it) all his assumptions about something and looked at it afresh. He would then see what was left. He found that consciousness "sees" a unity in things. For example, when he looked at one side of a box (forgetting what was in it and what it was used for), his mind still anticipated the whole box.

Husserl applied the same method to abstract notions such as time (by bracketing calendars, clocks, timetables, and the like). He found that time is experienced as eternal "now," in a flow from the past to the future – like hearing a single note, but knowing it is part of a song. Likewise, space is always "here" – wherever a person happens to be. Both "here" and "now" are personal to each individual consciousness, but everybody experiences time and space in exactly the same way.

MARTIN HEIDEGGER (1889–1976)
Heidegger studied under Husserl at Freiburg University and later succeeded him as professor. He borrowed Husserl's method and placed it firmly on the road to existentialism (see Sartre on pages 44–45).

HEIDEGGER AGED 70

READ MORE ON PAGE 60

DEWEY

Dewey was born in Vermont.

He was very close to his brother and they enjoyed outdoor activities like canoeing.

His mother made sure her sons had college educations.

Dewey said the more important lessons about life are learned outside the classroom.

Dewey's father didn't have much money because of his generosity toward the needy.

His father owned a grocery store.

Dewey traveled all over the world.

He opened an experimental school to test his ideas about teaching.

Dewey thought that parents should be involved in education.

He wrote two books that revolutionized teaching methods in the US.

I N THE LATE 1800s THE US DEVELOPED ITS OWN SCHOOL OF THINKING, KNOWN AS PRAGMATISM, which holds that ideas are only useful if they can be put into action. The Americans cleaned out the philosophy cupboard and threw out everything that had no practical value. One of the leading lights of this new age of practical thinking was John Dewey. He saw education as the most useful means of putting his ideas into practice. Education shaped society. Dewey passionately believed:

HEGEL (1770–1831)
At first, Dewey embraced Hegel's theory that the developing ideas of a divine mind are what form reality. Later he believed that nature itself is the ultimate reality.

"THE FULL DEVELOPMENT OF INDIVIDUALS AS HUMAN BEINGS"

The old pioneering spirit was very much alive in Dewey's home town of Burlington. The children he mixed with at school came from all walks of life. No one was deemed better than anyone else. This helped shape his whole outlook. Throughout his long life he was a strong believer in democracy. He stuck up for anyone he thought was getting a raw deal. The young Dewey loved learning about things, but he found school boring. This experience also shaped his future.

Dewey believed that society was the sum total of the people in it. The better educated the people, the better society would be. But bad teaching methods were resulting in a lot of potential going to waste. Dewey thought children's talents and interests should be taken into account, rather than just teaching them to parrot back facts. As head of philosophy at the University of Chicago, he got the chance to put theory into practice. He opened an experimental school. Dewey encouraged parents to take an active role in their children's education.

Dewey's reputation earned him invitations all over the world. He was especially popular in China and Russia. Unfortunately, his sympathetic view of the new Communist regime in Russia got him labeled a "red."

Toward the end of his life he was also in trouble with some educators, who thought his methods had caused standards to slip.

THE CHICAGO SCHOOL OF THOUGHT
At the University of Chicago, Dewey taught that ideas were tools to solve problems in the environment. This was hailed as a new philosophy.

LEON TROTSKY
Dewey took part in an official inquiry into Trotsky, a leader of Russia's revolution (1918). Dewey's study of all the evidence convinced him that violent revolution could never be justified.

TROTSKY IN 1920

READ MORE ON PAGE 59

WITTGENSTEIN

Wittgenstein studied to be an engineer. He invented a propeller.

In the First World War, he shunned a commission and fought as an ordinary soldier, winning medals for bravery.

He had a passion for watching second-rate cowboy films.

He stayed in a hut in Norway for two years working on logic and living like a hermit.

He said his philosophy was like a ladder to climb and then discard.

He finished writing his first major work of philosophy while he was a prisoner of war.

He was very secretive about his work and kept it locked in a safe.

Wittgenstein lectured at Cambridge University reclined in a deck chair.

He inherited two fortunes and gave them both away.

During the Second World War he worked as a medical orderly, believing simple work was virtuous.

L

UDWIG WITTGENSTEIN'S BURNING AMBITION WAS TO BRING AN END TO PHILOSOPHY, AND HE considered that he had done so – twice. He was brilliant, charming, arrogant, rude, witty, brave, and frequently suicidal. Equally as confusing is his philosophy. In fact he seemed to be two different philosophers, the older one disowning the work of the younger one. However, both of them agreed that language gives a picture of the world:

"THE LIMITS OF MY LANGUAGE ARE THE LIMITS OF MY REALITY"

BERTRAND RUSSELL
This philosopher was Wittgenstein's mentor and got him into Cambridge University. The pupil was soon teaching the teacher.

ALICE IN WONDERLAND
Wittgenstein loved Lewis Carroll's books about Alice. Carroll's use of words shows how language often adds up to complete nonsense.

Born in Vienna in the era of Freud, Wittgenstein was the son of a very rich steel magnate. Genius and emotional instability were family traits. Three of his four brothers committed suicide. The other lost a hand in the First World War, but he still succeeded as a concert pianist. Persistence was also one of Ludwig's major characteristics.

He launched into philosophy after studying logic with the English philosopher Bertrand Russell. Logic was Wittgenstein's tool. His aim was to solve all the traditional philosophical problems. In his first work he claimed to do just that. He said he was a businessman, like his father, and he was doing away with the business of philosophy.

Wittgenstein simply divided what could and could not be spoken about with any meaning. He said that language could only reflect the real world. So it was illogical to speak about God or the other big philosophical questions because they lay outside human experience.

As a philosophy lecturer, his eccentricity was legendary. His rooms were bare apart from a safe, in which he kept his notes. He lectured in a deck chair – ordering his students to bring their own. After class, he would rush off to the movies, where he sat in the front row and watched any old film, trying to forget the futility of his profession.

WITTGENSTEIN'S HOUSE
To take Wittgenstein's mind off killing himself, his sister asked him to build her a house. His obsession with perfection drove the builders crazy.

ALAN TURING
The only student to dare to contradict Wittgenstein was Alan Turing. He went on to invent the computer and to help England win the Second World War by cracking Germany's Enigma code.

READ MORE ON PAGE 62

SARTRE AND DE BEAUVOIR

Sartre met de Beauvoir in a café while they were both philosophy students in Paris.

Sartre said that people who lived stereotypical lives weren't really living at all.

Sartre wrote about the German occupation of France in the Second World War.

De Beauvoir said that women were oppressed by mundane chores and invisible in the world of philosophy.

De Beauvoir refused the conventional female role for herself.

Sartre enjoyed putting on stage productions.

Sartre wrote many plays and also acted in them.

He liked drinking and smoking and hanging out in cafés.

De Beauvoir wrote a book about female oppression called *The Second Sex*.

Sartre and de Beauvoir edited a left-wing newspaper.

SARTRE AND DE BEAUVOIR MET AS UNIVERSITY STUDENTS AT THE SORBONNE IN PARIS. THIS WAS THE start of a love affair that lasted 50 years. Famous the world over as the odd couple, they never married or shared property. They lived in hotels and ate in cafés. But they did share a common philosophy. Their particular brand of thinking is called existentialism – so named because it focuses on individual human existence. The idea is that only people are creative. They are free to rise above their creaturehood and create their own lives. Sartre said:

SORBONNE
De Beauvoir believed that education was very important. It gave women the chance to break free from oppression by using their "brain power."

NOBEL PRIZE
In 1964 Sartre was awarded the Nobel prize for literature for his novel *The Words*, but he refused to accept it, probably because he thought the award was only open to a select few.

"MAN MAKES HIMSELF"

De Beauvoir would probably have said that, once again, there was no mention of woman. Although de Beauvoir never had children of her own, she is known as "the mother of feminism." Her book *The Second Sex* was the first real attempt to explore why women allowed themselves to be dominated by men. Like Sartre, she came from an upper-class family. But the de Beauvoirs lost their money. When the servants left, the domestic chores fell on her mother, who resented her lot but never questioned that housework was a woman's duty. The young de Beauvoir wasn't slow to notice the unfairness of it all. She thought people should be free from prejudices about the sexes.

Sartre saw life as one gigantic stage, and people were the actors condemned to a lifetime performance. However, people are free to write their own "scripts" and cannot blame anyone else for a "bad performance." Those "actors" who allow themselves to be pushed into a role by others are denying that they are free to choose. In de Beauvoir's case this would have been behaving in the way society expected women to behave. The stars on life's stage are those who accept their freedom and make their own choices. They always take responsibility for their actions, whether these bring success or disaster.

WEATHER MAN
Sartre was in the meteorological corps in the Second World War and was taken prisoner by the Germans. He spent his time putting on plays in the prison camp.

SARTRE AND POLITICS
All his life, Sartre tried to reconcile his philosophy of personal freedom with his political beliefs. He supported the collective struggle against oppression.

READ MORE ON PAGE 61

PHILOSOPHY TODAY

TALKING ABOUT IT
One of the most important changes in philosophy today is the emphasis put on words and how they reflect the world.

PHILOSOPHY TODAY BEGAN WITH A SHIFT AWAY FROM "I" AS THE KEY TO UNDERSTANDING REALITY. Instead, thinkers started probing into human "structures." Language, science, and society itself all came under scrutiny.

FOUCAULT
FOO-KOE

FRENCH THINKER MICHEL FOUCAULT WAS INTERESTED IN THE WAY THE PAST IS colored by social attitudes. He dug into the history of thought and exposed the changing face of human nature. Foucault pointed out, for example, how disturbed people were once viewed as prophets and treated with respect. Today they are viewed as mentally ill, and are sometimes isolated by society.

DERRIDA
DERR-EE-DAH

JACQUES DERRIDA WAS BORN IN ALGERIA, STUDIED IN FRANCE, AND NOW works in California. He invented a way of thinking called "deconstruction." Derrida cast doubt on the very tools used to describe all philosophical thought – words. He "deconstructs," or pulls apart, language to show how there can be no fixed meaning. Words get in the way of the search for truth.

POPPER
POPP-ER

KARL POPPER LEFT VIENNA FOR ENGLAND IN THE 1930s. HE BECAME A "SIR" in 1965. Popper said science, far from being precise, was all just guesswork. He said you can believe a thing is true only if it can be proved to be untrue. His "falsification" method begins with provable truths like "There is a white cow in the field." If true, this can falsify statements like "All cows are brown."

KUHN
KOON

LIKE KANT BEFORE HIM, THOMAS KUHN'S WORK WAS CALLED A REVOLUTION in thinking. American philosopher Kuhn said that scientific research is not objective. It depends on its historical framework. This limits the field of evidence available to science. For example, scientists once thought the Earth was the center of the universe, then along came Copernicus with another idea.

FEYERABEND
FAY-AIR-UH-BEND

DESPITE BEING CRIPPLED BY A WAR WOUND, PAUL FEYERABEND WAS NOTED FOR his jolly personality. He thought philosophy should not be taken too seriously. Until he studied with fellow Austrian Popper, Feyerabend believed that science was the basis of knowledge. He later called all science theoretical, saying scientists defend their beliefs just like an ancient tribe defending its gods.

READ MORE ON PAGE 59, 62, 63

HORKHEIMER
HORK-HIME-ER

MAX HORKHEIMER WAS THE FIRST DIRECTOR OF A GERMAN INSTITUTE FOR social research, which opened in 1924. Its members used philosophy to examine and explain the present state of Western society. They were especially interested in the power money played in society and the success of Fascism. This group of thinkers became known as the Frankfurt School.

ADORNO
UH-DOOR-NOE

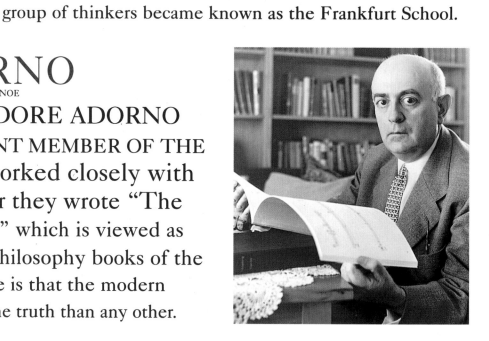

MANY THINK THEODORE ADORNO WAS THE MOST BRILLIANT MEMBER OF THE Frankfurt School. He worked closely with Horkheimer and together they wrote "The Dialectic of Enlightenment," which is viewed as one of the most important philosophy books of the 20th century. The main theme is that the modern "age of reason" is no closer to the truth than any other.

MARCUSE
MAR-KOO-ZA

HERBERT MARCUSE STUDIED UNDER HUSSERL AND HEIDEGGER (WITH WHOM HE fought) before he joined the Frankfurt School. He became the most politically active member of the group. Marcuse mixed Marxism with Freudian psychology. The result was a surprisingly optimistic view of the future. He thought technology would free people from the oppression of hard, boring work.

SCHOOLS OF PHILOSOPHY

THE PHILOSOPHERS FEATURED IN THE FIRST SECTION OF THIS BOOK FOLLOW A CHRONOLOGICAL ORDER, from the beginning of Western philosophy up to the present day. In this section of the book, these philosophers are looked at in the context of their ideas. Many philosophers have shared similar ideas, often because they have been influenced by the thoughts of those who have come before them. It is therefore possible to group philosophers into different schools of thought. It can be argued that there are hundreds, if not thousands, of these schools. This section describes some of the most important schools in Western philosophy. All the philosophers featured in the first section of the book belong to one of these schools – all, that is, except Socrates.

SOCRATES – THE FATHER OF WESTERN PHILOSOPHY

CONTINUED FROM PAGES 12–13

Socrates was not the first philosopher in the West. However, his importance to Western philosophy can be gauged by the fact that the early Greeks who preceded him are known as the Pre-Socratics, meaning "before Socrates."

Socrates is a bit of a mystery figure. He wrote no books. Most of what is known about him comes from his student Plato. The fact that Socrates died for his beliefs was an inspiration to all those later philosophers who have dared to challenge the status quo. Socrates was different from the ancient Greeks before him in that his concern was morality, or what was good, rather than what glued together the physical universe. Socrates wanted to find universal definitions for ideas such as good, justice, and wisdom rather than just descriptions. He thought that there must be some common denominator, or essence, in each of these abstract ideas. He knew that by being able to describe, for example, an act of courage, people must be able to recognize the essence of courage within that act. His quest was to isolate that essence.

Socrates' method of finding the truth about things was a system of questioning people's beliefs. Through this he hoped to reveal inconsistencies. He thought that the truth could only be found with a lot of hard work. The most influential group of philosophers at the time of Socrates was the Sophists. These people made their living, for the most part, teaching the skills of public speaking. Socrates did not regard them as philosophers at all. By his method of continual questioning, Socrates exposed their methods as little more than shallow gimmickry – twisting words to win an argument rather than revealing the truth.

THE PRE-SOCRATIC PHILOSOPHERS

The pre-Socratics were the first philosophers in the West. They are classed as the school that started Western philosophy off on its 2,500-year-old history.

THE EARLY GREEKS
CONTINUED FROM PAGES 8–11

THE ANCIENT GREEKS believed in a family of gods, who lived in palaces at the top of Mount Olympus, the highest mountain in Greece. The whole universe and its workings were attributed to the acts of these gods. Thales, Anaximander, Anaximenes, Pythagoras, Heraclitus, Parmenides, and Empedocles were part of a diverse group of pre-Socratic thinkers. One idea they shared was the desire to figure out what reality actually is. They dared to look beyond religion for an explanation, using the power of thought to try to discern the truth behind reality. This quest for the truth was the beginning of Western philosophy.

Parmenides was the first philosopher to rely on his mind rather than his senses. Like the early Greek thinkers before him, he believed reality is composed of one substance. The substance he imagined was unchanging and everywhere. His substance was seamless and without holes. This led him to conclude that motion is an illusion.

Parmenides' pupil, Zeno of Elea, went on to "prove" that motion is impossible by a series of paradoxes, or philosophical riddles. The most famous is a story about the athlete Achilles and a tortoise. Achilles decided to race the tortoise, but to make things fairer he gave it a head start. The problem is that, once he has given the tortoise a head start, he will never be able to catch up. For once Achilles reaches the point where the tortoise was, the tortoise will have moved on. When Achilles reaches this next point, the tortoise will have gone farther, and so on *ad infinitum*. The distance between them will get smaller and smaller as they advance, but it will never disappear. However fast Achilles runs, he can never catch up.

The early Greeks appeared to have thought themselves into a dead end with the idea that the universe is made of one unchanging, motionless substance. Empedocles was the first of a new group of philosophers known as "pluralists," who reasoned that reality must be made of more than one thing, namely fire, air, earth, and water. The second was Anaxagoras, who thought that Empedocles' theory of "four elements" was too simple. He said that the universe is composed of infinite "seeds" and that everything in the world contains seeds of all the elements, but in varying proportions. Anaxagoras was followed by the "atomists," a group who believed that reality is made of minuscule unchanging particles. The ceaseless grouping and regrouping of these particles into different patterns explained both change and motion.

GREEK SCHOOLS AFTER SOCRATES

After Socrates' death, three new schools of thought were founded in Athens. All of them were influenced by Socrates' search for what is good.

THE CYNICS

STARTED BY ANTISTHENES, a disciple of Socrates, the Cynics became widely known through the antics of Diogenes, Antisthenes' pupil. Diogenes preached that the only path to happiness was living simply and being virtuous. He exhibited a great contempt for riches by living in a wooden tub like a dog. This is how the cynics got their name. Cynic comes from the Greek word meaning doglike.

THE STOICS
CONTINUED FROM PAGES 18–19

TODAY, STOICS are people who face adversity with courage and dignity. For Zeno, the founder of the Stoics, these qualities encapsulated a whole way of life. To live virtuously meant rising above passion, to view pain and pleasure with indifference, and to help others. This was the way to true happiness. Zeno said that people's actions were the best guide to their real characters. He pointed out that nature had given him two ears but only one mouth, and so it was better to listen than to speak. He urged his followers to study their motives and actions each day, so that they could reflect on their mistakes and regulate their future conduct accordingly.

The Stoics were the first philosophers to believe in cosmic reason at work in the universe. They argued that everything happens for a reason and that there is no such thing as chance. The Stoics were the first "Determinists." They believed that there is no such thing as free will.

THE EPICUREANS
CONTINUED FROM PAGES 18–19

LIKE ZENO, the philosopher Epicurus also sought inner peace through living a good life. However, he and his followers rejected the idea of fate. The original Epicureans were not hedonists (people who live for pleasure). Epicurus's idea of pleasure was the avoidance of pain. He wanted to free people from the fear created by ignorance and superstition. He accepted the atomists' view that all things were composed of tiny particles. He taught his disciples that dying was nothing to fear because their atoms would simply be redistributed throughout the cosmos after death.

THE IDEALISTS

Idealists believe that the external, material world is produced by the mind or ideas and that it cannot exist separately. Reality therefore begins inside the head, not out in the street.

PLATO
CONTINUED FROM PAGES 14–15

PLATO thought that everything in the material world owes its existence to a perfect, eternal, and unchanging idea from which it is modeled. He called these ideas "Forms." Forms of abstract notions such as courage and justice serve as ideals for people to strive toward. Just as we can imagine an ideal horse, perfect in every way, we can imagine the ideal of justice and strive toward achieving it.

Plato's "dialogues" are usually about the nature of one Form or another. *The Symposium* (meaning "party with wine") is a discussion between different people on the nature of love. One person suggests that love between two people is like a circle cut in two, each making the other whole again. One of the characters, named Socrates, argues that true love is not a physical thing. He says it is when people search together for the truth and what is good. Socrates is often the main character in Plato's dialogues. It is usually safe to assume that whatever the character Socrates says is what Plato believed. "Platonic love" is a love that involves the mind and not the body.

In his dialogue *The Meno*, Plato examines the nature of knowledge. He argues that the mind, or soul, has passed through many existences, both in and out of bodies. Knowledge is about remembering this previous experience.

The most famous of Plato's ideal Forms is his ideas of an ideal society, which he wrote about in *The Republic*. In this book, Plato expresses strong views about the structure of society. He believed that there are different types of people. Some are not particularly bright and can never expect to hold important positions. He said these people have souls of bronze, and grow up to be farmers and other workers. Plato labeled this class "common people." Above them are those with silver souls. These people possess some talents and have the ability to become quite important in society. They are best suited to police and protect the state. Plato called this class of people "soldiers." At the top of the ladder are those with souls of gold. These people have the intelligence and education needed to become philosophers and rulers. Plato called this ruling class "guardians."

Plato argued that philosophers make the best leaders because they are wise and less likely to act irrationally. Plato believed that the state would remain stable and just with philosophers in power. His ideal society is an ordered class structure, where people remain fixed in their roles. People are trained to the limit of their ability, and that is their allotted place in life. It would be improper for a farmer to rule the state, or for a philosopher to work the fields.

Plato thought women and men are equally capable of ruling. But he also thought that men tend to do things better. However, his view on the equality of women and men was revolutionary for the time.

Plato's ideal state is a controlled society. The temptation to be greedy – one of society's greatest ills – would be removed by abolishing private property. To prevent people from making the state less important than their families, all children would be taken away at birth, never to know their real parents. Children would be raised by the state and encouraged to think of everyone as their mother and father. The state rulers would also choose people's marriage partners.

Many of Plato's ideas on the perfect society have influenced politicians throughout history. *The Republic* is still read by many people today.

HYPATIA

CONTINUED FROM PAGES 20–21

HYPATIA was a Neoplatonist, one of a number of philosophers living in the first few centuries AD who were strongly influenced by Plato's ideas. She shared Plato's belief that the material world is less real than the world of mind or spirit. Her idealism centered around a belief in a divine being, called "the One." She made a clear distinction between body and soul, matter and spirit. A person's soul is the only part that belongs to the world of spirit. It is like a small light in the dark, guiding a person toward true enlightenment, which can only be found in "the One."

GEORGE BERKELEY[1] (1685–1753)

BERKELEY denied the existence of a material world altogether. He said it is all in the mind. Berkeley argued that all we can know for sure is that we perceive things in our minds and that we believe them to exist outside of us. He said, "to be is to be perceived," meaning that things exist only by way of the mind's awareness of them. His critics scoffed at this notion. It would mean that things disappear when no one is looking. Berkeley, an Anglo-Irish bishop, had an answer for this. He said that God perceives all things and this is enough to guarantee their continued existence.

GEORG WILHELM FRIEDRICH HEGEL

CONTINUED FROM PAGES 34–35

HEGEL developed a massive philosophical system to explain reality. He maintained that the universe and everything in it is interconnected. He said that reality is the product of a cosmic mind. It is an idea in motion. All of history can be explained by the development of that idea. Hegel said that history could not be understood unless each age is viewed as a small piece in a huge jigsaw puzzle. This is a radical view of history. The traditional view is that history is the result of changes in the material circumstances of people. For instance, a new technology can change the way people communicate or fight wars. According to Hegel, these material changes in society are the effects of a deeper process of change. He argued that this deeper process is "an idea realizing itself."

Hegel said that this cosmic idea develops by way of a fixed pattern, which he called the "dialectic." This is a three-fold process. First of all an argument, or "thesis," is put forward. Then an opposing argument, or "antithesis," is introduced. After much struggle a compromise is reached, which is known as the "synthesis." This compromise then becomes the new "thesis," and the whole process starts again, *ad infinitum*. In Hegel's view, each great era of world history begins as the synthesis of opposing forces in the preceding era. These opposing forces (thesis and antithesis) eventually destroy the historical moment, but a new and better era rises from the ashes.

The "dialectic" is the motor by which Hegel's system operates. He demonstrated that the dialectic process underpins all history, including the history of human thought. Hegel argued that in each successive age, people develop a better knowledge about the world. Today, Hegel's proof of this development would be that modern science and technology give a more accurate picture of how the universe works than they did fifty years ago. In the future, that knowledge will have developed further.

For Hegel, history is progressing toward complete knowledge. The dialectic process will end in a final "synthesis" that reveals the mind of God.

THE MATERIALISTS

The materialists hold the complete opposite view to the idealists on the nature of reality. Materialists believe that everything that exists is either matter or depends on matter for its existence. The real world is out in the street, not in the head.

ARISTOTLE
CONTINUED FROM PAGES 16–17

ARISTOTLE was Plato's first great critic. Aristotle thought that Plato had gotten things backward by saying the "form," or idea, of a thing is what is most real. He said that material things are what is real and that their form is a part of their reality. Aristotle said that reality is made up of a lot of different things, which he called "substances." Any substance is a fusion of "thisness" (what it is made of) and "whatness" (its form, or what it is). For example, the "thisness" of a wooden chair is the wood from which it is made. The wood is shaped, or formed, into what it is – a chair.

Aristotle also found fault with Plato's Forms in that they did nothing to explain how things change. This led Aristotle to develop his own theory about change. He said that every substance has inherent "potentiality." By this he meant that things have within them the potential to change. For instance, water has the potential to become ice. It can also become steam.

Aristotle also disagreed with Plato's idea that the soul is separate from the body. He argued that all living things have a soul. This is what animates them and makes them different from substances like rock or water. The type of soul something possesses corresponds to what it does and what it needs. The lowest organisms, such as plants, need only to be nourished and to reproduce themselves. Animals have feelings, and so there is a sensitive aspect to their souls. People are much more complicated and have many more dimensions to their souls. Aristotle believed that living things are different because their souls are made of different stuff. He also thought that souls perish when living things die. However, he did identify an aspect of the human soul that might survive death. This aspect is thought or reason. Aristotle could find no physical basis for the thoughts that impose themselves on (or "inform") the mind.

Like Socrates, Aristotle thought people should strive to be good. He came up with a "means test" so that people could hone their virtues. He argued that real virtue lies between overdoing something and not doing it enough. For instance, being courageous is the mean average between being foolishly fearless and being cowardly.

This "golden mean" is also reflected in Aristotle's view on politics. Unlike Plato's belief in elite philosopher-rulers, Aristotle believed that a strong middle class should be in charge, so creating a balance between tyranny and democracy.

Aristotle's inexhaustible inquiry into the world around him led him to develop the first system of logic in Western philosophy. He wanted to develop argument into a tool to test the truth about things. The central feature of Aristotle's method is the "syllogism." A simple example is this: All men are mortal. Socrates is a man. Therefore, Socrates is mortal. This shows how two indisputably true statements can be used to produce a conclusion.

KARL MARX (1818–1883)

MARX was very influenced by Hegel. However, he disagreed with Hegel's view that history is the result of a developing idea. Marx thought that history is a material process. He argued that changes in the way people live lead them to develop new ideas, not the other way around.

Marx agreed with Hegel's view that history goes through different stages. He believed that the latest stage of history, capitalism, would be overcome. Marx dreamed of a better society in which money would not rule and everything would be shared. One of his most famous texts is *The Communist Manifesto*. In this short book he argues that capitalism makes slaves of people. He called people working for money "wage slaves," who are forced to produce goods they will probably never use.

THE SCHOLASTICS

The Scholastics were Christian thinkers who tried to understand and explain Christian doctrines in the light of ancient Greek philosophy. The Christian thinkers who lived in the first few centuries after the birth of Christ were known as "Church Fathers." Scholasticism dominated Western philosophy for hundreds of years.

ST. AUGUSTINE (354–430)

ST. AUGUSTINE was born in North Africa and studied in Italy. He was much influenced by Plato's ideas. Augustine sought to combine his Christian faith with reason. He thought that understanding is a reward of faith. He believed that the human soul holds latent within it certain ultimate and eternal truths.

Augustine was very interested in the nature of time. He said that time began for us when God created the world. This posed the question of God's existence before time. Augustine's answer was that God dwelt in an eternal present, outside earthly time. This led Augustine to the theory that "now" is all that really exists. The past is a present memory, and the future is a present expectation. This view allowed Augustine to stress the importance of what people *are doing* for God, not what they *will do*.

ST. ANSELM (1033–1109)

ST. ANSELM started the trend in Scholastic philosophy to try to prove the existence of God through rational argument.

Anselm, who became the Archbishop of Canterbury, invented several different proofs of God's existence. The most famous is called the "ontological argument," which he said came to him in a vision after breakfast. The reasoning behind God's existence is this: God is the greatest object of thought. If we say that God does not exist, then we can imagine something even greater – a God that does exist. Therefore God must exist. This argument was accepted over the centuries by many different philosophers, including Descartes, who came up with his own version.

ST. THOMAS AQUINAS

CONTINUED FROM PAGES 22–23

THOMAS AQUINAS criticized Anselm's "ontological argument." Among other things, he argued that it was beyond human reason to know the essence of God. Instead he came up with five proofs of his own to show that God exists. The first proof is that change is everywhere, so something must cause it. (It must be God.) The second proof is that things happen, so there must be a cause. (God, who is the first cause, must cause things to happen.) The third proof is that everything in nature is interdependent. (How can this be explained without coming to the conclusion that there is a God who is independent of nature?) The fourth proof is the question of harmony in nature. For instance, who gives fish their gills so they can breathe in water? (Only God could do this.) The fifth proof is the degrees of excellence that can be observed in nature. (This implies the notion of perfection and therefore a perfect being – God.) Aquinas set down these proofs in his book *Summa Contra Gentiles* (Against the Errors of the Infidels), the first of two massive volumes that he wrote. The intention of this first book was to prove to non-Christians through reason the importance of being a Christian.

THE RATIONALISTS

Rationalists consider that truths about reality can only be revealed through reason, not by believing what the senses tell us about the world.

PARMENIDES

CONTINUED FROM PAGES 11 AND 50

PARMENIDES can be considered the first Rationalist because he thought that the material world could only be properly understood by thought and reason, not what is perceived through the senses.

Parmenides' ideas have survived in fragments of a long poem he wrote. The poem has two main themes: "The Way of the Truth" (what reason tells us about the world) and "The Way of Seeming" (what our senses tell us). Parmenides argued that thinking and being (existing) are one and the same, meaning that it is impossible to think of a thing that does not exist. His logic was that "nothing" can only be thought about if it is thought of as "something." Therefore nothing, or "not being," is not possible – there can only be "being." In the same poem, Parmenides reasoned that time is an illusion. He said that the past and future do not exist since they can only be thought of in the present.

RENÉ DESCARTES
CONTINUED FROM PAGES 24–25

DESCARTES is credited with being the first "modern" philosopher. He broke the hold of Scholasticism on philosophy by questioning everything he had been taught. Descartes was a scientist. This gave him the desire to establish a deductive system of knowledge that would give him logical, necessary truths about the universe.

In his book *The Meditations*, Descartes set out to discover a firm foundation for his system. He realized that everything he knew had been learned from his senses. But he questioned whether it was sensible to trust a known liar. How could he trust his senses when, for example, an oar looks bent in water? Descartes's method was to doubt everything systematically. All that was left was the secure knowledge that he could think, even if he was only dreaming that he was thinking. This was the foundation for his new system of knowledge. The first deduction that he could make from this indisputable truth was that, by virtue of thinking, he must exist. However, he had thought himself into a philosophical corner. How could he prove that the outside world also existed? How could he now trust what he perceived about the world? The sole solution was to prove the existence of God – only then could he deduce that his own God-given senses could be trusted. Many philosophers consider that Descartes's thinking went downhill at this point.

Descartes came up with two arguments for God's existence. The first was that he (Descartes), by virtue of his doubts, was an imperfect being. However, imperfect as he was, he could still entertain the idea of a perfect being – God. Only a perfect being could be the cause of such a perfect idea. Therefore, God must exist. Descartes's second argument is a variation on St. Anselm's "ontological" proof. Descartes argues that the idea of a perfect being contains perfection in every degree. Therefore the idea of God must contain God's existence. Having "proved" God's existence, Descartes no longer needed to consider that the world might be the product of an evil genius. He reasoned that a perfect being would not allow such a state of affairs.

Descartes still had to know how he knew about the world. As a thinking being he reasoned that his God-given senses would not deceive him if they were properly employed. He deduced that it was mind, or reason, that told him the truth about the world. When he melted wax, it looked, felt, and smelled different, but in his mind he was in no doubt at all that the substance was still wax.

The building block of Descartes's rational system was his assertion "I think, therefore I am" (from the Latin: cogito ergo sum). By this, Descartes had identified mind as something separate from matter. In this sense, he is known as a "dualist" philosopher, meaning that he thought that the world consisted of two separate substances: mind and matter. The essential property of the mind is consciousness, whereas the essential property of matter is "extension" in space, in that it has length, breadth, and depth. In his view, all matter, including the human body, is "mindless." All living things are just matter in motion. This dualist philosophy left Descartes with the problem of explaining how the mind and body united to become a person. He theorized that the double impressions received by virtue of having two ears, two eyes, two hands (and so on) united with consciousness in a gland in the brain. This theory was hotly debated, even before his death, and Descartes himself was aware of the unsatisfactory nature of this conclusion. One of those who questioned his theory was Queen Christina of Sweden. She also disagreed with Descartes's view that animals were mindless, having observed her own much-loved pets.

BARUCH SPINOZA
CONTINUED FROM PAGES 26–27

LIKE DESCARTES, SPINOZA believed that reason was the true source of all knowledge. Like Descartes, he was brilliant at mathematics and geometry and agreed that philosophy should try to copy their methods of deduction. Spinoza's aim was to construct a "geometry of philosophy." In his most important book, *The Ethics*, he tries to demonstrate by means of a mathematical system how to lead a good life. The foundation of Spinoza's system is the indisputable truth of God's existence. Everything else in Spinoza's system develops from this. He arrived at this truth by way of trying to solve the problem posed by Descartes's belief that the universe consisted of two substances: mind and matter. Descartes called them "finite substances." Beyond these is God, the "infinite substance." Spinoza felt that this was contradictory.

Spinoza agreed with Descartes's definition of substance, which is something that does not depend on anything else for its existence. But Spinoza felt that Descartes should have stopped once he identified God as the "infinite substance," because an "infinite substance" would also possess all the properties of the "finite substances" – so how could these exist independently? In this way, Spinoza was able to argue that God is not separate from the rest of the universe, as Descartes (and nearly everyone else) had thought. Rather, God and the universe are one and the same. Spinoza insisted that God and nature are one substance and that mind and matter are just different forms in which God appears. Spinoza thought that there might be many other ways in which God appears, but that human senses are too limited to perceive them. Spinoza's belief in one substance makes him a "Monist."

Spinoza was also a "Determinist," in that he believed that everything that happens in the world is part of a divine plan. This might seem to negate the possibility of freedom in Spinoza's system. But Spinoza disagreed. He thought that the only way to be free is for people to accept what they are. Spinoza believed that knowing ourselves clearly is part of coming to understand God. This makes sense in terms of Spinoza's system because, if God is everywhere and everything, each person is a part of God. Spinoza said that the more people understand their relationship to the rest of the world, the more free they will feel. The realization that there is no randomness is liberating because it frees people from being ruled by their emotions. To Spinoza, it was not "reasonable" to feel anger if someone hurt you. There was no point. It would not change a thing. A person with a clear understanding of the world (and therefore of God) accepts whatever happens.

For Spinoza, the happiest people are those who put God first – not a God that exists as a higher being, but the sum total of everyone and everything in the cosmos. In this way, Spinoza thought he had invented a perfectly rational form of ethics. People who act unselfishly are happy in the sure knowledge that they are leading good lives.

GOTTFRIED LEIBNIZ[1] (1646–1716)

GERMAN PHILOSOPHER LEIBNIZ was the last great rationalist philosopher. Unlike Spinoza, who thought there is only one substance, Leibniz believed that the universe is made up of an infinite number of substances, each one unique. He called these substances "monads" and argued that each monad reflected everything else in the universe.

You can visualize what Leibniz meant – just think of a mirrored ball. If you look at a mirrored ball, you see your reflection and what is in the space around you. However, instead of just reflecting the immediate surroundings, Leibniz's monads reflect the entire universe. This means that everything in the world is connected to everything else. Instead of thinking about the world as a complex jumble of space, time, and matter, Leibniz introduces the idea that each moment and place is connected to every other. No monad is unconnected.

However, Leibniz also argued that monads do not act upon each other. Instead, he said that each monad was set upon its course from the beginning. According to Leibniz, everything that exists and happens exists and happens for a reason. For there to be no reason, Leibniz reasoned, would be irrational. This was the building block of Leibniz's system of thought. Like many philosophers before him, Leibniz traced the cause of "everything that is" back to God. It was God who set in motion the myriad monads that make up reality, and each monad carries within it all that it will ever be.

Leibniz called this idea that everything is programmed in advance by God "preestablished harmony." Leibniz reasoned that this world is just one of an infinite number of possible worlds, but because God chose to bring it into existence, then it is logical that this must be the best of all possible worlds. This is because God is a perfect being and so would never have chosen anything but the best.

THE EMPIRICISTS

Empiricism is the complete opposite of rationalism. Empiricists believe that true knowledge of the world is obtained through the senses, not by reason. These philosophers argue that we have ideas only because we have perceptions. All knowledge is based on experience.

JOHN LOCKE
CONTINUED FROM PAGES 28–29

LOCKE disagreed with Descartes's rationalism and had no inclination to rely on religion to support his thinking, as Descartes had done.

His most important book of philosophy was called *An Essay on Human Understanding*. In this book Locke tries to demonstrate how people acquire knowledge. He described philosophers as the "underlaborers" of the scientists, because a philosopher's job is to clear the ground of the obstacles to gaining knowledge.

The first issue Locke grapples with in the book is whether people are born with ideas or whether these are acquired through experience. He argued for experience. According to Locke, the mind of a newborn baby is a blank slate. From then on, the mind is bombarded with a massive input from the senses. Locke called these first impressions about the world "ideas of sensation." These might include experiencing the color yellow or the weight of an

apple. They are "simple" ideas, which cannot be broken down any further. If someone does not understand yellow, it can only be shown, not explained. Simple ideas are the building blocks of all knowledge. To begin with, these ideas are passively received by the mind. Then the mind reflects on them. The mind becomes active when it begins to combine them into "complex" ideas. For example, a unicorn is a combination of simple ideas. Locke called this type of idea "complex" because it has no basis in reality as perceived by the senses.

Locke was challenged by those who said his theory did nothing to explain whether reality is in fact real, or just a set of ideas caused by the senses. Locke tried to answer this by making a distinction between a thing's primary and secondary qualities. Locke argued that all things in the outside world have qualities that are part of the thing itself and cannot be separated. For example, if we close off all our senses to an orange so that we cannot smell it, taste it, see its color, or feel its shape, the orange still has shape, weight, and density. Locke called these types of qualities "primary." The orange's color, taste, and smell are all "secondary" qualities. Locke said that secondary qualities are produced in the mind in response to the stimulation of our senses. In this way, Locke felt he had proved that there is a real external world, and that a thing's existence did not depend on our perceptions.

Locke's "real" world full of things and their primary qualities is very similar to Descartes's idea of material substances (see page 53). Locke was then faced with the question of whether this objective world of things is all that there is. He conceded that there must be a more basic "something" – and he admitted that he didn't have a clue as to what it is!

DAVID HUME
CONTINUED FROM PAGES 30–31

HUME used a two-pronged method for testing the truth about reality. This is often referred to as Hume's "fork." On one prong of the fork are all the truths that are the logical conclusion of reasoning. These include all mathematical calculations (such as 3+2=5) and self-evident truths (such as the statement "all women are female"). Hume argued that reason, therefore, tells us very little about the world. On the other prong of the fork are what Hume called "matters of fact." These are all the things we learn about the world through direct experience. Like Locke, it was Hume's view that all useful knowledge about the world comes from what is experienced through the senses.

Hume used this two-pronged approach to sift through all possible ideas about reality in search of the truth. He found that his fork picked up very little that would answer any of the big questions in philosophy, such as "Is there a God?" When Hume applied his method to this question, he found that the concept of God could not be linked to direct experience. Therefore the existence of God could neither be proved nor disproved.

Hume said that people could be certain of very little. His method led him to be skeptical about everything that failed his test – even previously accepted laws of nature. For instance, he argued that we cannot be certain about our belief in cause-and-effect. His most famous example is one billiard ball striking another and causing it to move. Hume could directly observe that one event followed another. He could also observe the first ball striking the other. But he could not observe the "cause," or the necessary connection between the two events, however many times he experienced the sequence. He said that we expect one ball to move if it is struck by another, but this does not necessarily mean that it always will. In the same way, he challenged the law of gravity. He said that we expect an object to fall if it is dropped because we have always observed that this happens. Hume claimed that the laws of nature are in fact just expectations imprinted in our minds, which we then project out into the world. These expectations are built up from our past experience of the world. If tomorrow we dropped a glass and it did not fall, then our belief in gravity would be destroyed. Hume's point was that past experience is no guarantee of future experience. He wanted to remain open-minded about the nature of reality,

which is why he adopted such a skeptical approach.

Another belief that Hume challenged was the idea that we can know who we are. According to Hume's method there can be no such thing as "self" in the sense of a continuing, unchanging identity. When he tried to look at himself from the inside, he always found himself in the process of feeling something, be it hot, cold, happy, or angry. At best, he found himself to be a "bundle of perceptions" that constantly changed. In other words, not only did he doubt that he stayed the same person throughout life, he doubted that he was the same person from one moment to the next! Hume said that only the blindness of familiarity kept people from realizing this about themselves.

Hume disagreed with the idea that morality is a question of reason. He said that it is our feelings that give us a sense of what is right and wrong. Compassion motivates us to help others or put other people's needs above our own. He argued that we cannot deduce what is good or bad from facts about the world. Judgment comes from within, by reflecting on our own feelings and empathizing. This accounts for the fact that different people have different moral values. Hume pointed out that it would be more "reasonable" to make cold decisions or to act selfishly. He said, "It is not contrary to reason to prefer the destruction of the whole world rather than the scratching of my finger."

IMMANUEL KANT
CONTINUED FROM PAGES 32–33

KANT was a Rationalist, never questioning the power of reason to deduce truths beyond human experience, until he encountered the Empiricist views of David Hume. Kant wrote that Hume woke him up from his "dogmatic slumber." However, Kant did not change camps and become an Empiricist. Instead, he took what was important from each school and put them together into one philosophy. This is known as "Kant's Synthesis."

Kant found Hume's skepticism challenging. Hume had concluded that knowledge beyond human experience is impossible and that experience could tell people very little for certain. Kant wanted to find a way out of this dire state of affairs. He began by trying to discover the capabilities of human thought. The result was his book *Critique of Pure Reason*.

His findings reversed Hume's claim that gravity and other "natural laws" are merely expectations caused by repeated experience. Kant argued that these laws are part of the construction of the human mind itself. In other words, people are already preprogrammed at birth with a set of rules to structure their experience of the outside world.

Kant was also interested in ethics. He disputed Hume's views that right and wrong are personal judgments based on experience. Kant believed he could provide a rational way to distinguish between good and bad actions. He argued that an action would be wrong if the result of everyone doing it caused a universal problem. For example, he considered it wrong to lie. Kant reasoned that if everyone lied, no one could trust the word of anyone, and the result would be disastrous. In the same way, an action is right if its general practice would be to the benefit of everyone.

KARL POPPER
CONTINUED FROM PAGE 47

POPPER wanted to solve the problem that Hume had left to philosophy. Hume had argued that whenever we think we are observing a law of nature, in reality we are just projecting our expectations onto the world. He said that our experience of the past is no guarantee of future events.

Popper realized that Hume's skeptical conclusion put the entire scientific method in doubt. Hume was putting science's belief in natural laws such as gravity on a par with a belief such as "all cows are brown" (using the scenario that no one has ever seen a cow that was not brown). Popper's aim was to try to restore faith in science.

Popper agreed with Hume that science cannot be a matter of certainty, but he disagreed that this made science useless. Through his method of "falsification" (see page 47), Popper showed that it is possible to prove some scientific claims wrong. In contrast, nonsciences like astrology cannot be

proved either right *or* wrong. However, each time science gets it wrong, it gets closer to getting it right. For example, if we have come to believe from our experience that all cows are brown, and then we see a white cow, we are adding to our knowledge of all the possible colors that cows might be. In other words, we are getting closer to the whole truth about the color of cows.

THE PRAGMATISTS

Pragmatism is a practical view of philosophy. Pragmatists view the truthfulness of an idea in terms of its usefulness in real life. This school was the first major movement in philosophy to come from North America.

CHARLES SANDERS PEIRCE (1839–1914)

PEIRCE invented the term "pragmatism." He meant it to be a method to clarify the relationship between thought and action. According to Peirce, ideas that have no concrete value in everyday experience are meaningless.

WILLIAM JAMES (1842–1910)

JAMES was very influenced by Peirce. He turned pragmatism from a general theory of meaning to a down-to-earth practical philosophy. He thought the truth of an idea lay in its "cash value," meaning that it is truthful if it is useful. James's pragmatism was subjective in that he recognized that the same idea could be useful to one person and not another. Although Peirce admired how James had turned his abstract theory into a full-blown philosophy, he tried to separate his original theory by renaming it pragmat-*ic*-ism. Peirce said that this word was "ugly enough to be safe from kidnappers."

JOHN DEWEY
CONTINUED FROM PAGES 40–41

DEWEY'S main influences were William James and the naturalist Charles Darwin – who published his theory of evolution in the year Dewey was born. Darwin's work made Dewey view consciousness as part of nature rather than a separate faculty. Dewey saw the mind as a problem-solving tool that continually adapts to the environment in the same way that creatures evolve different characteristics.

Dewey thought that as an organism became more complicated, so did its capacity to deal with its environment. First of all there is instinctive behavior. Later, habits develop. When habits fail to deal properly with situations, then an organism develops the ability to reason, or to think what to do. Dewey maintained that all thoughts are just ideas for action. This way an organism gains knowledge about the world.

THE PHENOMENOLOGISTS

Phenomenology is the study of how things appear. The Phenomenologists tried to get behind the surface of how things appear to reveal the nature of consciousness itself.

EDMUND HUSSERL

CONTINUED FROM PAGES 38–39

HUSSERL was the founder of phenomenology. He wanted to do away with theories about reality and restore certainty to philosophy. His method was to describe exactly how reality presented itself to consciousness. He wanted to make philosophy into a precise science. He believed that until this happened the traditional sciences had no firm foundation and could never be certain of what they were doing. Husserl's philosophy begins at what he called the "natural standpoint," the everyday world as experienced by each person. His method is to perform a "phenomenological reduction" of that experience. This involves ignoring all previously held personal, philosophical, and even scientific assumptions about a thing and then examining what remains. The aim is to disclose exactly how the mind works. Husserl believed that it is possible to step back and perform a phenomenological reduction on consciousness itself. He called this "pure" consciousness that could observe "everyday" consciousness at work, the "transcendental ego." This would be the starting point of all knowledge.

Only a small percentage of what Husserl wrote has been published. Most of his work still lies unpublished in an archive in Belgium.

MARTIN HEIDEGGER[1] (1889–1976)

HEIDEGGER was Husserl's most famous pupil and he worked as Husserl's assistant. Heidegger's main interest was existence (or "being") itself, based on the fundamental philosophical question "Why is there something rather than nothing?" In his most famous book, *Being and Time*, Heidegger uses Husserl's method of phenomenological reduction to describe human existence. However, Heidegger's version of phenomenology does not separate the outside world from individual human consciousness. He argued that we cannot separate ourselves from the world. We are first of all "beings-in-the-world." Heidegger invented a lot of new, hyphenated words because he felt that language was too limited to describe human experience. Heidegger identified "care" as the characteristic that separates humanity from the rest of existence. By that he meant the active concern people demonstrate about everything they perceive, such as family, pets, politics, events of the past, and what will happen in the future.

MAURICE MERLEAU-PONTY[2] (1908–1961)

MERLEAU-PONTY borrowed a lot of Husserl's ideas. His basic disagreement with Husserl's phenomenology was that it is based on mental rather than bodily experience. In his first major book, *The Phenomenology of Perception*, Merleau-Ponty argued that how we use our bodies determines how we experience the world. Like Kant he believed that all our ideas come from sense impressions that are shaped by certain rules of understanding. But he disagreed that these rules are purely mental. He believed that our understanding is shaped by rules of the body. In this early book, he demonstrated how people whose bodies have been damaged or impaired experience the world differently.

THE EXISTENTIALISTS

The Existentialists believe that there is no order in the universe and no objective right or wrong. Individuals are free to create their own lives according to the choices they make and must take responsibility for their actions.

[1]HI-dig-ger [2]MER-LOE-pohn-TEE

Søren Kierkegaard[1] (1813–1855)

Kierkegaard is seen by many as the father of existentialism because of his attack on Hegel's view that individuals are less important than their historical context. The Danish philosopher rejected Hegel's system of an unfolding process, which left people with little or no free will. According to Kierkegaard, philosophy begins and ends with individual human existence. He believed that people are free to choose their experience and that it is morally wrong to shirk this responsibility. He urged people to be true to themselves when making life's choices, which he viewed as leaps of faith.

Jean-Paul Sartre
CONTINUED FROM PAGES 44–45

Sartre studied phenomenology with Husserl and was also influenced by the ideas of Heidegger. Sartre developed phenomenology into existentialism. Heidegger had talked about "inauthentic" people, meaning those who refuse to accept responsibility for their existence. Heidegger felt that facing up to the finality of death ought to make people value their existence and make something of their lives.

For Sartre, true existentialists are "authentic" people. They face reality head on and take control of their lives. The ability to choose and act is the basis of human freedom. Sartre rejected the idea of an external authority, such as God or cosmic reason, to guide people. He saw this as an illusion created to comfort desperate minds. Accepting responsibility for choices can make the moment of decision full of anxiety. For Sartre, this was the price of freedom.

Sartre explored his ideas in *Being and Nothingness*, his most famous book. The title reflects two modes of existence that Sartre had identified in the world. A thing that exists just by "being" there, like a pebble on a beach, exists "in itself." By contrast, consciousness is "no thing." It exists "for itself." It is capable of becoming involved in the world. Most people act as if they are pebbles on a beach, unable to change themselves or the world around them. Existentialists challenge the limits of their situations by living "for themselves."

Feminist Philosophers

Feminists believe that society is based on an unequal division between men and women. The "first wave" feminists were concerned with equality between the sexes. "Second wave" feminists are more concerned that what is special to women be recognized and valued as important.

Mary Wollstonecraft[2] (1759–1797)

Wollstonecraft's most influential book, *A Vindication of the Rights of Women*, was published in 1792. It called for the abolition of the inequalities between men and women. At this time women could not vote or own property. They belonged to their husbands. Wollstonecraft argued that "mind has no sex," and so women should be entitled to complete personal and economic freedom. For her trouble she was called a "hyena in petticoats" and a "philosophizing serpent."

Her daughter, also named Mary, married the poet Shelley and wrote the novel *Frankenstein* (1818).

Simone de Beauvoir
CONTINUED FROM PAGES 44–45

De Beauvoir's book *The Second Sex* (1949) began the second wave of feminism. The book shows how men are seen as normal and women as the negative "other" or "second" sex. De Beauvoir argued that this view of women dominates all aspects of society and influences how women are treated and how they treat themselves. She said that "One is not born, but rather becomes, a woman." De Beauvoir wanted to expose the male mask that Western philosophy has worn over the centuries.

Luce Irigaray[3] (1939–)

Irigaray agrees with de Beauvoir's view. As a practicing psychoanalyst, she has been influenced by Freud's work. However, she took exception to Freud's idea that women envy men's genitals and so view themselves as lacking what it takes to be a male. Irigaray believes that women's oppression goes beyond past and present economic and social structures. She argues that language itself is male-oriented and so can never express what it is to be female (a simple example is that God is referred to as *He*). Irigaray feels that women are forced to speak a language that does not value or represent them. She calls for the creation of a new, more fluid, feminine form of language, capable of reflecting woman's multidimensional nature.

THE POSTMODERNISTS

Postmodernism is a relatively recent movement in philosophy. It was so named because it began as a reaction against the "modern" age of philosophy since Descartes. Descartes had begun the trend in establishing systems aimed at discovering fixed and absolute truths about the universe. The Postmodernists' view is that philosophy is fooling itself. Postmodernism is a broad school, and there are differing opinions about which philosophers belong in it.

HERACLITUS
CONTINUED FROM PAGE 10

HERACLITUS lived more than two thousand years ago, but his ideas are truly "postmodern." This is because Heraclitus believed that the only thing that remains constant in the universe is that everything changes. Therefore, Heraclitus was the first Western philosopher to suggest that we can never have knowledge that lasts for all time.

FRIEDRICH NIETZSCHE
CONTINUED FROM PAGES 36–37

NIETZSCHE rejected the idea of any higher truth. He said, "The apparent world is the only world: the 'real world' is merely a lie." He agreed with Heraclitus's view that the world is constantly changing. For Nietzsche there is only flux and chaos, which can be creatively forced into shape through individual will. He believed that all claims to higher knowledge are lies based on self-deceptions. He thought that language is one of the biggest deceivers of all. He pointed out how limited and distorting words can be. For example, referring to things collectively as trees, leaves, flowers, houses, and so on promotes similarities and suppresses differences. Nietzsche felt that any beliefs we have about the

world are just useful devices for dealing with life. However, he thought the belief that every action has a cause leads to the false belief in a higher self. He said, "A thought comes when *it* will, not when *I* will."

LUDWIG WITTGENSTEIN
CONTINUED FROM PAGES 42–43

It is Wittgenstein's later, rather than early, work that can be viewed as postmodern. The young Wittgenstein had thought that he'd found certainty and precision in language. In later life, Wittgenstein disagreed intensely with his earlier self. The older Wittgenstein thought that all meaning in language depends upon how words are used. He talked about "language games," meaning that language has certain rules of usage just like any game. He said that when the rules were broken "language goes on vacation." Wittgenstein was very fond of the children's books *Alice in Wonderland* and *Alice Through the Looking Glass*. They are packed full of examples that show how meaning can be turned upside down when the rules of language are broken. For instance, a promise for "jam every other day" is never fulfilled because it never is "every other day."

According to Wittgenstein, any philosophical claim to knowledge of absolute truth is nonsense, a perfect example of "language on vacation."

THOMAS KUHN
CONTINUED FROM PAGE 47

KUHN was the first philosopher to question the existence of fixed truths in science. He argued that the truth that scientists uncover is only relative to the times in which they live. Kuhn claimed that scientists cannot escape their historical conditioning. Their thinking is limited by the sum total of the knowledge available to them. This historical conditioning is similar to Kant's goggles (see page 33). Scientists cannot help but view reality from a certain perspective. Every now and then a major discovery will cause a change in perspective (which Kuhn called a "paradigm shift"). However, science's old goggles are simply replaced by a new set. It did not mean science was getting any closer to the truth.

MICHEL FOUCAULT
CONTINUED FROM PAGE 46

FOUCAULT believed that our view of the past changes from one age to another. The way we think about history is never neutral or without bias. Foucault stressed the central role power plays in our understanding of the past. The old saying "history is written by the victors" means that only those in power get their version of events heard. Foucault's work shows that there is no continuity in history. The rules that structure society and govern people's lives are constantly shifting. And those who set the rules are those who hold the power.

Foucault was also interested in "micropower." This is power operating on a much smaller scale. He showed how prison, school, and hospital authorities exert power over the "inmates" by a system of rules. Those who disobey the rules are punished.

Foucault's excavation of the past gave him little hope for the future, since technological advances offer vast possibilities for the misuse of power.

JACQUES DERRIDA
CONTINUED FROM PAGE 46

DERRIDA'S ideas are similar in many ways to the later ideas of Wittgenstein. Derrida agrees that the meaning of words depends on how they are spoken or written. He believes that the way we understand ourselves and our language changes over time. Nothing is fixed.

A key word for Derrida is "difference." He maintains that everything differs from everything else. For example, a certain word in a book has a different meaning in that book than in any other. And within any book, a word has a different meaning in different chapters.

Derrida argues that philosophers who claim to have discovered fixed and absolute truths about the world are unaware of the tricks that language plays on their own writings. When Derrida writes about these philosophers, he "deconstructs" their claims by uncovering these tricks. Deconstructionism has become a popular movement beyond philosophy, influencing architects and even fashion designers.

GLOSSARY

Atomism *The idea that the universe is made up of tiny particles.*

Determinism *The belief that everything that happens in the universe is fixed in advance.*

Dualism *The belief that the universe consists of two different things (mind and matter).*

Empiricism *The belief that experience is the source of all knowledge.*

Ethics *A branch of philosophy that tries to answer questions about right and wrong.*

Existentialism *The idea that people create themselves and their experience by the choices they make.*

Extension *The way in which an object fills up (extends into) space.*

Hedonism *The belief that pleasure is the most important thing in life.*

Idealism *The view that the material world is produced by the mind.*

Logic *The study of what constitutes a sound argument.*

Materialism *The view that matter is the only substance that exists and that the mind cannot exist independently from matter.*

Monism *The belief that the universe consists of one ultimate substance.*

Ontology *The study of what kinds of things actually make up the universe.*

Paradigm shift *A change in the framework within which scientific theories are constructed.*

Paradox *A statement that contradicts itself. A well-known example is the Cretan who says, "All Cretans are liars."*

Phenomenology *The study of how things appear (as opposed to how we think they appear).*

Pluralism *A belief that reality is composed of more than one basic substance.*

Pragmatism *The view that the truth and value of ideas depend on how useful they are in real life.*

Rationalism *The theory that truths about reality can be deduced by reason alone.*

Skepticism *A belief that it is impossible to know anything about the world with certainty.*

Syllogism *A deductive argument made up of three statements, the last of which is the logical conclusion of the other two.*

INDEX

ACKNOWLEDGEMENTS

The publisher would like to thank the following for their kind permission to reproduce photographs:
a=above; b=below; c=center; l=left; r=right; t=top

AKG London: 7tr, 27cr, 27br, 39cr, 39br, 45cr, 47tl, 48cr, 48bl; Lessing / Collegium Maius Library, Krakow 5tl; Lessing / Kunsthistorisches Museum, Vienna 37tr; Lessing / Louvre, Paris 15br, 19cr; Lessing / Metropolitan Museum of Art, New York 13br; Kunsthalle, Hamburg 17br; Museo di San Marco, Florence 5cl; Ancient Art & Architecture Collection: 4cla; Annie Cohen – Solal: 45crb; Associated Press AP: Alan Mothner 4br; Bildarchiv Preussischer Kulturbesitz: 48tl; Bridgeman Art Library: Bibliothèque Nationale, Paris: Portrait of Confucius (c.551–479bc), 17th century 4bc; Bibliothèque Nationale de Cartes et Plans, Paris: Astrolabe, copper, by Ahmad Ibn Khalaf an Iraqi Arab, 9th century 21crb; Musée des Beaux-Arts, Rouen / Peter Willi: Alexander and Diogenes, 1818 by Nicolas Andre Monsiau (1754–1837) 19tr; Musée Carnavalet, Paris / Roger-Viollet, Paris: The Execution of Louis XVI, 21 January 1793 by Danish School (18th century) 33crb; Museo del Castello, Sforzesco: Portrait of John Calvin (1509–1564) by Ary Scheffer (1795–1858) 27tr; O'Shea Gallery, London: The Marble Watch Tower or Lighthouse Erected by Ptolemy Soter on the Island of Pharos, near the Port of Alexandria 21tr; Phillips, The International Fine Art Auctioneers: Thomas Aquinas being received into the Dominican Order, c.1500 by German School (16th century) 23br; Private Collection: Trial of Galileo, 1632 by Anonymous 25br, An Eyewitness

Representation of the Execution of King Charles I (1600–49) of England, 1649 by Weesop (fl.1641–49) 29tr; Scottish National Portrait Gallery, Edinburgh: David Hume (1711–76), 1766 by Allan Ramsay (1713–84) 33tr; York City Art Gallery: Oliver Cromwell by Edward Mascall (c.1627–fl.75) 29cra; British Museum: 13cra; Camera Press, London: 46cr; Corbis - Bettman: 31br; E.T. Archive: 15cra, 21br, 23tr, 25cra, 33br, 35br; Mary Evans Picture Library: 4tl, 4cl, 15crb, 17tr, 17cr, 19br, 23cra, 31tr, 31cr, 33cra, 35tr, 39cr, 41br, 43cra; Explorer 35cr; Foto Leutner-Fachlabor: 43crb; Hulton Getty Picture Collection: 41cr, 43tr, 45tr; The Ronald Grant Archive: Superman (1978) © DC Comics 7cl; Sonia Halliday Photographs: 37cr; Image Select: 41tr; Lebrecht Collection: 37br; Magnum: Bruno Barbey 45br; Martine Franck 46bl; Moviestore Collection: Terminator 2: Judgement Day (1991) © Guild 6tl; Museum of London: 25tr; Peter Newark's American Pictures: 29crb; NYT Permissions: Jim Wilson 47cr; Oxford Scientific Films: Konrad Wothe 6br; Photo Jean-Loup Charmet: 21cra; Science Museum: 25br; Science Museum / Science & Society Picture Library: 43br; Science Photo Library: BSIP Laurent 7bl; Mehau Kulyk 5cb; Laguna Design 6cr; Petit Format / Institut Pasteur / Charles Dauguet 5br; Ph. Plailly / Eurelios 6cl; US Department of Energy 6tr; Studio Kontos: 13tr; Telegraph Colour Library: Spencer Rowell 46tl; Lin White: 15tr. Special thanks to Nicola Liddiard for pictures of her grandmother on page 3.

The publisher would also like to thank Csanad Siklós and Jo Bartlett for their help with research, Lynn Bresler for the index, and Dawn Sirett for her editorial input.